BANGALORE - MYSORE

Sangam Books

Material compiled by AFRIED RAMAN

Illustrations: G.B. Anand and V.N. Barathan
Cover illustration: Sathiamoorthy
Maps by CARTOGRAPHY DEPT., Orient Longman Ltd., Hyderabad

We thank
– Survey of India, Dehradun
– The Ministry of Defence, Government of India

Sangam Books Ltd., 1994
57, London Fruit Exchange
Brushfield Street, London E1 6EP

By arrangement with Orient Longman Ltd.,
3-6-272 Himayatnagar,
Hyderabad 500 029 (A.P.), INDIA

First Published 1994

ISBN 0 86311 431 8

Phototypeset by
Art Prints
105 Luz Church Road, Madras 600 004

Printed in India by
NPT Offset Pvt. Ltd.,
231 Royapettah High Road, Madras 600 014

Disha Guides

BANGALORE – MYSORE

CONTENTS

BANGALORE

MYSORE

Note : Every effort has been made to provide an up-to-date text, but changes are constantly occurring and we will be grateful for any information about changes you may notice.

Bangalore — Introduction

There is a well known story about a great Hoysala king, Veera Ballala, who lost his way during a hunt and was fed boiled beans by an old woman who had nothing else to offer. 'Bangal-uru', the place of boiled beans, is now the fifth largest city in India.

Bangalore's history is as lively and effervescent as the life that it enjoys today. According to legend Kempe Gowda I of Yelahanka, a feudatory under the Vijayanagar kings, was once out on a hunt and was surprised to see a hare chase his dog. He was convinced that a city built on that spot was bound to flourish. He thus founded a township on this 'gandu bhumi' or heroic land.

There is also a less fanciful explanation for the origin of the word Bangalore. In Kannada, 'bengallu' means granite and 'uru' is town or place. 'Bengallu uru' (town of granite) could have, in the course of time, become Bangalore.

Kempe Gowda built a strong fort around the fledgling hamlet. Despite his valiant efforts the walls kept crumbling. Finally to overcome what seemed to be divine objection, the idea of human sacrifice was suggested. Kempe Gowda's daughter-in-law, Lakshmidevi, is said to have made a secret offer of her life to the gods. In this manner Bangalore's fort and future were saved.

As Kempe Gowda had envisaged, Bangalore's enviable location and material prosperity made it a bone of contention. The neighbouring feudatory chiefs, jealous of Kempe Gowda's growing power and wealth, turned their Vijayanagar suzerain against him. He then imprisoned Kempe Gowda for five years.

In 1759 a warrior from the ranks of the Mysore army shot into prominence. Hyder Ali Khan, a military genius, played a powerful and memorable role in the history of India and of Bangalore in particular.

By the time Hyder Ali came to power in 1761, Bangalore had been besieged several times, conquered twice and even bought once (for a price of Rs 3 lakh by Chikka Deva Raja Wodeyar). Throughout this turbulent period, however,

Bangalore continued to grow and flourish. Hyder Ali, who was determined to rid his kingdom of the presence of the British, launched a war against them. His son, the great Tipu Sultan, carried on this crusade against the British until he was defeated in the Fourth Mysore war in 1799 at Shrirangapattana. Though their reign was short and bloody, Hyder Ali and Tipu Sultan played an important part in shaping the history of Bangalore. The city's military associations are still very much in evidence. This can be seen in its war memorials and many church walls studded with commemorative plaques.

Bangalore's pleasant climate and scenic countryside have made the city a favourite place to live and work in. Bangalore is an 'industrial city'. It is the country's fastest growing metropolis and has many industries manufacturing machine tools, aircraft, computers and electronics. Large corporations such as Hindustan Aeronautics and Indian Telephones are in Bangalore.

Bangalore is also called the 'garden city'. The centre of the city is beautifully laid out with wide tree-lined avenues, graceful buildings and green parks which have earned it this title. Bangalore has a wide range of shops which sell an amazing variety of things — fashionable readymade garments, moderately priced shoes and sandals, light silk fabrics and sarees, and all kinds of woodwork.

Films buffs in Bangalore have a choice of over 90 cinema halls which screen films in many languages. The city has three large and many small auditoria which are always crowded for there is nothing the people here love so much as a good play, dance or music concert, be it in the Western, Carnatic or Hindustani style. Bangalore's enthusiastic audiences and roomy stages have made it a favourite venue for national and international performing troupes.

Not far from Bangalore and well connected by road and rail are other places of interest. From Mysore, (the seat of the Wodeyar kings), the exquisite temples of Belur and Halebid, and the Jain pilgrimage centre of Shravanabelagola are easily accessible by road and rail. To the north lies Hampi the ruins of the capital of Vijayanagar which bear testimony to the glory of one of the mightiest empires in India.

Gazetteer

Bangalore's major historical and architectural sights are scattered widely within the limits of the city. However, for the convenience of the sightseer, it can be divided into the following zones.

The old city and its numerous extensions (west and south of the Vidhana Soudha) and the cantonment and civil areas with its extensions (east of the Vidhana Soudha and north of the Corporation Offices of the city). The sights mentioned in the Gazetteer are listed in a logical order. As a further aid a star system has been adopted:
* interesting
** recommended
*** highly recommended

This will enable the tourist, if pressed for time, to see the most interesting (historical or architectural) places in each zone.

Distances mentioned in the guide are measured from the Vidhana Soudha which is centrally located as the reference point. Map references are provided in bold type to the right of each entry heading. The number **B2 14,** for instance, refers to square B2 of the map on page 14.

Distance from airport to Vidhana Soudha - 10 km
City Railway Station/City Bus Station - 3 km
Cantonment Railway Station - 1.5 km

Bangalore has an adequate though not very reliable bus service but without a bus route map getting around would be a tedious business. The metered three-wheeler cabs called autorickshaws are ideal as they are easily available, affordable and allow a greater degree of flexibility in one's sightseeing programme. Taxis are expensive by Indian standards and particularly so in Bangalore as drivers rarely go by the meter and demand arbitrary fares.

THE OLD CITY AND ITS EXTENSIONS

(west of the Vidhana Soudha and south of the Corporation Offices)

In the seventeenth century Chikka Deva Raja Wodeyar (who according to an astrological prediction would become the King of Mysore after Dodda Deva Raja) is said to have bought Bangalore from the Mughal general Kasim Khan of Sira for a sum of Rs 3,00,000. His first task was to build a citadel to protect the township contained in the old fort. This fort, enlarged by Hyder Ali, was badly damaged in the four wars against the British. Its remains, however, can still be seen today.

Further south along Krishnaraja Road is Tipu Sultan's palace situated next door to the beautiful Venkataramanaswamy temple. Its position near the sultan's palace demonstrates the unusually secular outlook of this heroic king and reflects the unique sense of harmony that existed during his reign.

To the west, in the mainly residential area of Kempe Gowda Nagar, is the unusual cave temple dedicated to Gangadheeshwara which was built by Kempe Gowda in the sixteenth century. The Bull temple, which was once situated on farm land, is now surrounded by sprawling housing colonies which have expanded far beyond Kempe Gowda II's prediction of the city limits.

* Mythic Society (1 km) **D2 161, A2 133**

Almost hidden by the public buildings that loom over it the Mythic Society on Nrupatunga Road is a haven for historians and book lovers. This voluntary public institution was founded in 1909 by, amongst others, a French missionary, a British collector and an Indian professor. The Society is housed in the Daly Memorial Hall (named after Sir Hugh Daly, Resident of Mysore and President of the Society for many years). It is a simple structure with Corinthian pillars and three arched doorways. The walls are lined with the portraits of many famous patrons including three generations of Mysore maharajas. The well-stocked reference library contains more than 10,000 volumes. The society offers free reading room services.

Mythic Society

* Dharmaraja Temple (2 km) B3 152

Of the four Dharmaraja temples in Bangalore the one in the vicinity of the Ulsoor gate in Nagarthapet (opposite the City Corporation Offices) is the most important. Built in the Dravidian style of architecture in the early nineteenth century the temple itself is not of particular interest. But every year, on an appointed full moon night during the 'basant' (spring) season, the 'Karaga' procession begins and ends in this temple.

This is a festival of the Tigalas, a tribe of enterprising agriculturists who migrated to Bangalore during the reign of Hyder Ali. The significance of the Karaga festival is fascinating. The festival's central theme is the worship of Draupadi, the daughter of Agni (the God of Fire) and the wife of the five Pandava brothers in the epic *Mahabharata.* Draupadi meaning 'shakti' or power was the motivating force behind the Pandavas' victory over their enemies, the Kauravas. The festival, therefore, is also a celebration of the triumph of good over evil.

The Karaga procession usually starts soon after midnight and ends at about six in the morning after stopping for prayer at the tomb of Hazarat Taukkal Mastan, a sufi saint who lived in the eighteenth century. The highlight of the festival is the dazzling sword play in a mock battle enacted by sword wielding Tigala men which, according to Sir Mark Cubbon, Commissioner of Mysore State from 1834 to 1861, is 'a harmless exercise and one that needs no license'!

* Sangin Jamin Masjid (Jumma Masjid) (3 km) **B3 152**

Amongst the busy crowded lanes in the Taramandalpet area behind the Ulsoor gate police station (close to the Corporation Offices) is a mosque, the only mark of the Mughal emperor Aurangzeb's ambitious attempt to conquer the south. It was constructed between 1687 and 1690 by the Mughal 'kiledar' (keeper of the fort) of Bangalore. Built over the ruins of a Hindu temple the tall ornamented granite pillars of the original structure can still be seen in the prayer hall. The mosque has been renovated in recent times and has therefore lost much of its original character.

* Ranganatha Temple **C2 161**

This small but gracious temple off Avenue Road was built by Kempe Gowda II. Despite considerable renovations the carved pillars in the 'navaranga' depicting the various avatars of Vishnu, and the 'garbha griha' (sanctum sanctorum) remain untouched. Of the several snake stones installed in the courtyard by devout worshippers one is believed to have been placed there by Kempe Gowda himself.

** Fort Area (4 km) **A3 160, C3 161**

When Chikka Deva Raja Wodeyar acquired Bangalore in 1687 Kempe Gowda's fort contained a flourishing township within it. To guard it from invaders Chikka Deva Raja built a smaller, oval citadel. In 1761 this was enlarged and rebuilt entirely in stone by Hyder Ali. It was designed by Hyder Ali's maternal uncle, Ibrahim Khan, who became the 'kiledar' (keeper) of the fort. It formed a formidable defence structure and was guarded by two large well fortified gates. The southern entrance called the Mysore gate was not as attractive as the Delhi gate in the north which looked out over the old 'pete' fort as it was called. Described as a handsome structure in the best style of Muhammedan military architecture the Delhi gate with its delicate plaster ornamentation is still visible (facing north towards the city market) from inside the fort.

The entrance to the fort is off Krishnarajendra Road. A terse plaque set into the fort walls marks the spot where the British forces broke through Tipu Sultan's defences on 21 March 1791 and defeated him in the Third Mysore War. Inside the fort, facing the entrance, is a tiny unadorned Ganesha temple with the royal double-headed peacock emblem of the Wodeyars in the pilaster on the wall above the roof. Although large portions of the fort were demolished over the years to make way for modern buildings some of the dungeons which housed British prisoners of war are still intact and are accessible from the battlements above.

** Tipu Sultan's Palace (4.5 km) **B3 160**

South of the Fort, on Krishnarajendra Road (near the Bangalore Medical College) stand the remains of Tipu Sultan's palace. In 1789 when it was completed the large airy palace built mainly of wood stood within the citadel walls. From the upper storey balconies the sultan held audience with his subjects seated in the hall below. The palace had a profusion of tall, fluted pillars and cusped arches. The mud walls and ceiling were painted with gilded Persian motifs, and the wooden ledges and balcony parapets were decorated with carefully carved beadwork.

From 1831 to 1868 Tipu Sultan's palace was used to house the State Secretariat till the Public Offices (Athara Kutchery) building was constructed between 1864 and 1868. Now only a portion of the original palace which Tipu Sultan called 'the envy of heaven' remains.

*Venkataramanaswamy Temple (4 km) **B3 160**

This temple is situated opposite the Bangalore Medical College on Krishnarajendra Road. It is the oldest monument in the fort area and was built by Chikka Deva Raja to commemorate his aquisition of Bangalore. The temple bears witness to many historic deeds of the days gone by. It has become a symbol representing the chaotic days of Chikka Deva Raja Wodeyar, and the spirit of the times of Hyder Ali and Tipu Sultan. Built in sand coloured granite, this exquisite Vishnu shrine is a perfect example of the Dravidian style of architecture. The 'vimana' (tower) containing the sanctum sanctorum is capped by a pyramidal 'shikara' with horizontal carved bands. The 'mantapa' (columned hall) is decorated with elaborately carved pillars and lion brackets. Around the walls on the outside are bas relief figures of Vishnu, Brahma and Shiva with their respective mounts as well as those of the saptarishis (seven legendary holy men) and saptamatrikas. Entry to the temple is from the Krishnarajendra Road.

*** Lal Bagh (5 km) **C1 169**

This famous garden is as synonymous with Bangalore as the Taj Mahal is with Agra. It was first laid out in the latter half of the eighteenth century and has been continuously tended for over 200 years. The first 40 acres were planted by Hyder Ali about a mile to the east of the fort. His son Tipu Sultan too was interested in horticulture. He added to and improved the gardens by importing shrubs and flowering plants from such far off places as Turkey, Mauritius and Persia. Hyder Ali's penchant for red roses gave the park its name 'Lal Bagh' which means red garden. This pleasure garden was laid out in the Mughal style with a separate plot of land for each kind of plant. These were meticulously tended by a versatile tribe of farmers called Tigalas (originally from what is today called Tamil Nadu). The broad gravelled walks and fountains ornament the park.

The Glass House, Lalbagh

In 1856 the Lal Bagh spreading over 240 acres was made into a horticultural garden and placed under the management of a superintendent from the Kew Gardens in London. A glass house modelled on the Crystal Palace in London was built in the Lal Bagh in 1890 and since then it has been the venue of many public functions. The garden today contains over a thousand varieties of tropical and sub-tropical plants and trees many of which belong to rare species.

Flower shows are held every year in January and August.

Peninsula Gneiss The Lal Bagh has a 3000 million-year-old geological specimen called the Peninsula Gneiss. This rock outcropping rises abruptly out of the ground. It was used 400 years ago by Kempe Gowda as a look out post as it offers a wide and excellent view of Bangalore city.

Kempe Gowda's tower Perched atop the rock is one of the towers of Kempe Gowda II denoting the southern boundary of his city. The other three are located near the Mekri Circle in the north, Ulsoor Lake in the east and on the southern bank of the Kempambudhi Tank in the west. **C3 145, C1 163, D1 167, and D1 169**

Bugle Rock, Basavangudi

** Gavi Gangadheeshwara Temple (6 km) **A1 168**

The Gavi (cave) temple is dedicated to Gangadheeshwara, an aspect of Lord Shiva. Its structure is completely different from other temples built in Bangalore during the reign of Kempe Gowda and his successors. The shrine itself is located in a low cave, the interior darkened by centuries of soot from burning oil lamps . A semi-circular pathway cut into the rock runs behind the main shrine. Beautifully carved statues, including one of Parvati, are set in niches. There is a rare idol of Agni, the God of Fire. Facing the shrine is a small 'Nandi' (bull), Shiva's mount. Between 13 and 14 January every year the rays of the setting sun pass directly between the horns of

Nandi and illuminate the Lingam (the idol) in the main shrine. This unusual temple was said to have been built by Kempe Gowda as an act of thanksgiving when he was released after being wrongfully imprisoned by his Vijayanagar sovereign. The location of the temple was perhaps deliberately chosen as a reminder of his years in prison.

** Basavangudi (Bull) Temple (6 km) B2 168

Located in the southern residential area of Basavangudi to which it lends its name, the Basavangudi ('basava' means bull) temple is one of the oldest temples in Bangalore dedicated to Nandi, the mount of Shiva.

This monolithic bull, about 4.5m tall (including the base) and about 6m long, is said to be older than the temple which houses it. According to folklore several acres of land were used to cultivate groundnuts in the fifteenth and sixteenth centuries. The farmers were often plagued by a solitary bull which would forage in the fields at night. At last a watchman deputed by the farmers lay in wait for the bull and when it appeared, killed it with a crowbar. The next morning, to the farmers' consternation, the carcass of the bull had been transformed into a giant statue. The crowbar can still be seen embedded in its back!

Every year a groundnut fair called 'kadelekayi parishe' is held in November and December soon after the harvest. The highlight of the fair is the offering of the newly harvested groundnuts to Nandi.

Kempe Gowda I built a simple temple around the statue. An inscription in the temple says that the source of the River Vrishabharati which runs to the west of Bangalore is at the feet of the statue.

Bugle Rock To the north of the Bull Temple is the Bugle Rock. Here a part of the Mysore army was regrouped under the leadership of Mir Khammar-ud-din on the eve of the final assault by the British army in the Third Mysore War. **B2 168**

* Indian Institute of Science (7 km) A3 144

In 1898 Sir Jamshedji Naoroji Tata, the famous industrialist, set aside Rs 30 lakh (three million rupees) as a trust for the creation of an Indian Institute of Science (IIS) along the lines of the Royal College in London. Situated on 372 acres of verdant land donated by Krishnaraja Wodeyar IV, J N Tata's dream took concrete shape when the first building was constructed in 1909. The main building which houses the administrative offices is a fine gray granite structure. The whole building cost Rs 11 lakh when it was built and this included the quaint brass door knobs and hinges imported from Birmingham.

The IIS is almost wholly a postgraduate university and actively encourages postdoctoral research in many branches of science and engineering. Each department is separately housed in attractive buildings. The carefully nurtured shrubs, flowering plants and tree-lined avenues with very little vehicular traffic add to the aesthetic appeal of the place. The institute has an excellent research library containing books and periodicals in the fields of advanced science and engineering.

Indian Institute of Science

In front of the main building is an interesting statue created by Gilbert Hayes in 1922. It depicts the founder dressed in the costume typical of his community, surrounded by four Roman figures—Jove with thunderbolts, Vulcan with an anvil depicting steel, Minerva with her distaff full of flax, and Calliope, signifying the founder's achievements in industry and keen interest in research and higher studies. From a bronze rail hangs the lamp of learning and there are cavorting dolphins on either side which indicate that the founder was widely travelled.

The Institute's alumni consists of many of the luminaries of the Indian scientific and technical establishments, like C V Raman, H J Bhabha and Vikram Sarabhai.

Raman Research Institute Close to the IIS is the Raman Research Institute founded by Sir C V Raman. **C3 145**

CANTONMENT AND CIVIL AREAS

(east of the Vidhana Soudha and north of the City Corporation Offices)

Established in 1537 Kempe Gowda's city was surrounded by a strong mud fort. Chikka Deva Raja added another fort in the seventeenth century to defend the first one. This in turn was strengthened by Hyder Ali in the mid-eighteenth century. The fort was later demolished by the British. The seat of power then shifted from the old town to the east where the British laid out parks and gardens and established their own buildings in the classical style popular in the latter half of the nineteenth century.

This zone therefore encompasses the two important centres of the city, one created by Kempe Gowda in 1537, and the other in 1833 when the British took over the administration of the Mysore state. Kempe Gowda's streets still exist and people continue to live in the 'petes' or old quarters established in the sixteenth century.

To the east in sharp contrast to the narrow twisted streets of the old town are broad tree-lined avenues fringing the green sprawl of Cubbon Park. Situated in and around the park at varying distances are many government buildings including the magnificent Vidhana Soudha from where Bangalore and indeed the whole of Karnataka is governed.

Further east is the popular shopping area of M G Road and Brigade Road. Towards the west lies what was then called the Cantonment Bazaar, a maze of streets and shops around the aptly named Commercial Street. Here there is the impressive St Mary's Church and a few mosques which are examples of old monuments still in use today. The area known as the Cantonment came into existence in 1809 when Shrirangapattana proved unhealthy for the troops stationed there after the fall of Tipu Sultan in 1799.

This zone encompasses a fascinating variety of eras, cultures and lifestyles. The spirit of co-existence that bridges these differences reflects an attitude that is typical of Karnataka.

In the east is the Ulsoor (or Halsur) Lake, a pleasant picnic spot close to which stand two of the oldest monuments in Bangalore—the Someshwara Temple built long before the city itself and the Kempe Gowda tower erected in the latter half of the sixteenth century. Since the time of Hyder Ali, this locality has traditionally had a large Tamil population who had migrated to find work in his gardens, and later during the rule of the British worked as contractors and builders. Road names like Narayan Pillai Street or Annaswamy Mudaliar Road, quaint old houses with beautifully carved door lintels and the Kannada language liberally interspersed with Tamil create one of the many distinctive cultural 'pockets' in Bangalore.

Northwest of Ulsoor Lake are 'tahe' (towns) built by European administrative personnel whose charming bungalows and flower-filled gardens with the spires of churches in the distance gives the place the appearance of an English village. Here the streets still proudly bear the names of long forgotten Englishmen, and Cavalry Road and Infantry Road are reminders of the city's role as a military station in the nineteenth century.

*** Vidhana Soudha (10 km from the airport, 3 km from the railway station) **D1 161, A1 133**

For over a century the public offices were housed in Tipu Sultan's palace and subsequently in the Athara Kutchery. Finally a building large enough to house the Secretariat as well as the State Legislature was constructed.

This giant granite edifice, located on the northern edge of Cubbon Park was built in 1956 at a cost of twenty million rupees. The Vidhana Soudha measures about 230m in length and 115m in width and is capped by a gigantic 20m dome on which stands the capital of Ashoka's Pillar. The carved stone pillars and giant sunshade over the main porch are distinctly Dravidian while the six smaller cupolas add an Indo-Saracenic touch.

The interior of the Vidhana Soudha has some fine specimens of woodwork. Of special interest are the sandalwood door leading to the Cabinet Room and the Speaker's Chair in rosewood, both beautifully carved and polished by craftspersons from Mysore.

Vidhana Soudha

** Athara Kutchery (High Court Building) (opposite the Vidhana Soudha) **B1 133**

The offices of the eighteen departments of the Revenue and General Secretariat ('Athara Kutchery' in Hindustani) grew to such a size that they could no longer be contained in Tipu Sultan's palace (which in 1831 had been the only building large enough to accommodate these departments). A new building was then constructed for this purpose.

This graceful two storeyed building in the European-classical style with Ionic columns housed the Public Offices from 1868 to 1956. It was also used as the Legislature. The Legislative Council used to meet in the imposing Central Hall. On the ceiling at the west end of the hall is a fine medallion portrait of Sir Mark Cubbon, the efficient and popular Commissioner of Mysore from 1834 to 1861.

When the legislators moved across the road to the Vidhana Soudha in 1956, the Athara Kutchery (as it is still called) became the High Court building. Painted a deep red with touches of white, the Athara Kutchery provides a perfect foil to the white, columned Vidhana Soudha.The equestrian statue

Athara Kutchery

of Sir Mark Cubbon located behind the building was designed by Baron Marochetti and erected in 1866.

* Cubbon Park (Chamarajendra Park) (Opp. Vidhana Soudha)

D2 161, A1 162, A1 133

The three hundred acres of Cubbon Park, as it is still popularly known, were laid in 1864 between the then clearly demarcated areas of the city and the Military Station (Cantonment) zone.

It was laid by Sir Richard Sankey of the Royal Engineers and named after Sir Mark Cubbon. Cubbon Park, unlike Lal Bagh, is not laid out in a formal style. The natural outcroppings of rock and the groves of shady trees and giant bamboo provide a pleasant retreat from the busy streets that surround it.

The Vidhana Soudha and Athara Kutchery (High Court) are situated on the northern edge of the park while the southern section is fringed by buildings of historical and educational interest.

The Jawahar Bal Bhavan Named after India's first prime minister whose affection and concern for children is legendary, the Bal Bhavan is located just within the Park precincts. The Bal Bhavan is a popular spot with children. It has a fairground and a theatre where children's films and plays are shown but the biggest attraction is the toy train, the Putani Express, which chugs around the park with carriages full of delighted children The Putani Express runs from *1500 – 1900; closed Mon and 2nd Sat. Tel: 564189* **A1 162 B2 133**

* **The Circular Aquarium** is situated next to Jawahar Bal Bhavan. It has about eighty varieties of aquatic fauna on display; *closed Tue.*

Putani Express

** Statue of Queen Victoria B1 133

Gazing haughtily down at the traffic is a statue of Queen Victoria situated at the junction of Kasturba Road and M G Road. This exquisitely carved marble structure, a replica of the Victoria statue in Worcester, stands 3.3m high on a pedestal of Mysore gray granite. Costing an enormous sum of £1000 in 1906 it was sculpted by Sir Thomas Brock.

Museum Complex A1 162, B2 133

Westward along Kasturba Road is the museum complex comprising the Visvesvaraya Industrial and Technological Museum, the Government Museum and the Venkatappa Art Gallery.

* **The Government Museum** is a neat building with white Corinthian pilaster capitals in the Renaissance style. Founded in 1866 it is one of the oldest museums in India.

The stone sculptures on the ground floor are mainly from the Hoysala period (c.1000–1300) famous for its delicate and elaborate carvings and detail. There are also a few pieces from Shravanabelagola, a famous Jain pilgrim place 160 km from Bangalore, and exhibits from the Paleolithic and Indus Valley periods. Of particular interest is the large model of Tipu Sultan's fort at Shrirangapattana and the handsomely decorated cannons which were used by his armies against the British.

First floor, eastern room The majority of the exhibits here are paintings of the Tanjore school in which gold foil and semi-precious stones are used to create an embossed effect. There are some exquisite miniatures from Rajasthan and Gujarat as well as a few fine examples of the Deccan Mughal style. A showcase containing rare beautifully crafted Indian musical instruments is of special interest.

First floor, western room This contains a largely undistinguished collection of natural history exhibits including stuffed birds, mammals and reptiles; *open 1000 – 1700; closed Wed.*

Venkatappa Art Gallery Flanking the Government Museum to the west is the Venkatappa Art Gallery named after one of Karnataka's most famous artists. Venkatappa belonged to a family of court painters and was skilled in various art forms all of which are displayed here.

The first floor contains work by contemporary artists mainly from Karnataka. Of particular interest are a sketch by K.K. Hebbar and an oil painting by M.F. Hussain, both well known Indian artists; *open 1000 – 1700; closed Wed.*

Visvesvaraya Industrial and Technological Musuem To the right of the Government Museum is the Visvesvaraya Industrial and Technological museum. It is named after M. Visvesvaraya, Dewan of Mysore from 1912 to 1918, who provided a stimulus to technological advancement in the state. The museum houses a comprehensive range of exhibits depicting motor power, electronics, uses and properties of wood and metal, and a section on popular science where visitors are encouraged to work on the exhibits to stimulate a deeper interest in them; *open: 1000 – 1700; closed Mon.*

* Public Library D2 161, A2 133

The attractive Seshadri Iyer Memorial Hall houses the Public Library. In front of the building is a lovely rose garden sloping gently towards the Hudson Circle. Within it on a polished black granite pedestal is the statue of Seshadri Iyer, Dewan of Mysore from 1883 – 1901. There is also the Jawahar planetarium close to the Raj Bhavan which is well worth a visit.

*** St Mark's Cathedral (1 km) A1 162

Looking at this lovely cream coloured cathedral in its calm surrounding it is difficult to believe that St Mark's, founded in 1808, completed four years later and consecrated by the Bishop of Calcutta in 1816, was said to be 'one of the ugliest buildings ever erected... with its yellow-washed walls and low roof, it resembled nothing so much as a Bryant and Mary matchbox!' But in 1902, a year after it was enlarged, the new tower fell in and in 1923 a fire destroyed the nave. Completely rebuilt in 1927 the church far from looking like a matchbox is a beautifully proportioned building. It has a graceful dome over a semi-circular chancel with rows of Roman arches along the church walls. The main porched entrance is to the south.

St. Mark's Cathedral

The semi-circular tympanels are set with painted glass each with a different floral pattern. The gilded flowers against the snow-white background of the dome within the chancel create a remarkable effect. Set in the eastern wall of the sanctuary are two small stained glass windows and a rosewood cross installed in 1939.

** St Mary's Basilica (1.5 km) **B3 152**

Although the present ornate Gothic-style church was built between 1875 and 1882 by Rev. L E Kleiner, St Mary's was founded much earlier when Abbé Dubois built a small chapel in 1818. A special feature of this church is the large number of stained glass windows said to have been brought from Paris by Rev. Kleiner. The windows were removed during World War II and carefully remounted after 1947. In 1973 the church was raised to the status of a minor basilica, the sixth in India, by a papal order issued by Pope John Paul VI.

Morning service 0600 and 0645.
Evening service 1430 in the Annexe.

* Commercial Street (2 km) **B1 162**

The Commercial Street area is one of the three most popular shopping areas in Bangalore the other two being M G Road and Kempe Gowda Road. Shops in Commercial Street offer a wide choice of goods: footwear, accessories, handicrafts, artefacts, readymade garments, fabrics and saris, bedding and furniture. Commercial street is also well known for furnishing fabrics and many skilled upholstery tailors have set up shop there.

* St Andrew's Kirk (1.5 km) **A1 162**

This is the only Scottish Kirk in Bangalore. The simplicity of this church is relieved by a large stained glass window depicting Christ and eight of his apostles. The Church also boasts of a pipe organ which was installed in 1881. Amongst the highly polished brass plaques around the walls is one in memory of John Cook, principal of Central College in Bangalore, who died in 1915.

* Russel Market (1.5 km) **B3 152**

This market is one of the best in Bangalore though certainly not the cheapest. It sells all kinds of flowers, fruit, vegetables and meat (camel meat too, at certain times of the year) all under one roof. It was built in 1926 on an old lake bed whose shady trees sheltered an open-air market even before the idea of Russel Market was mooted. Designed by W H Murphy, the executive engineer of the municipality (civil area) and named after an Indian Civil Services officer T B Russel (who took a keen interest in the project), Russel Market was formally opened in 1927 in a 'lavish ceremony' that cost Rs 269.80.

The market opens every morning at six. Inside, the pyramidal mounds of fruits and vegetables and the attractively arranged flowers entice a large crowd of buyers.

** St Francis Xavier's Cathedral (3 km) **B3 152**

Close to St John's Church and westwards along St John's Church Road is the impressive grey granite Roman Catholic Church of St Francis Xavier. The stark, vaulted Byzantinesque interior is illuminated by stained glass windows set high above in the short transepts. This church is architecturally very different from the other churches in Bangalore and therefore well worth a visit; *Sunday service: Holy Communion: 0630 – 0845.*

* United Theological College (2.5 km) **A2 152**

Off Miller's Road close to the Cantonment Railway Station is the attractive campus of the United Theological College founded by J. Duthie of the London Missionary Society. When the college began to function in 1910, the first of its kind in India and perhaps in the world, it was supported by several mission societies which were active in India. The curriculum laid great emphasis on high quality ecumenical theological education. Its syllabus today contains not just Christian and Church doctrine but also the study of Sanskrit, Marxism and Buddhism.

The campus contains classrooms and hostels for men and women, the Charles Ranson auditorium, residential quarters for the staff and married students, and a large, well catalogued library. The UTC library contains Asia's largest collection of theological material. Numbering over 60,000, many of the books are manuscripts and rare ecclesiastical books. Amongst its collection is also a full set of Mahatma Gandhi's 'Harijan', a 1726 Tamil Bible translated by Danish missionaries, palm leaf manuscripts about 750 years old and a complete photocopy of a fourth century Greek Bible—the original of which is in the Vatican.

** Holy Trinity Church (2.5 km) **C2 163**

This was the second church to be built in Bangalore (after St Mark's Cathedral). The Holy Trinity was the direct result of the report of Colonel Sims of the Madras Engineers to the Directors of the East India Company, where he requested that they build another church since the existing one could barely accommodate 500 people. This resulted in the Holy Trinity Church being built.

It was designed by Major Pears in the classical style. The large porch is supported by ten Ionic pillars. There is an unusual bell made in London in 1847 which still tolls for the Sunday service. Under the foundation stone laid in 1848 is a bottle containing a few coins, specimens of six different types of grain and a parchment record of the event. Completed in 1851 the Holy Trinity was an archetypal military church. The walls in the nave are studded with a number of tablets commemorating a number of military men and women. There are many memorials to young officers who succumbed to the Bangalore climate in spite of its reputation as being salubrious!

The bronze and marble tablets are in themselves worth the visit. Elaborately ornamented, they sport regimental crests, cannons, scrolls and even a haughty bust of a Major General Clement Delven Hill who died fighting in the Peninsula campaigns in 1845. Mosaic tiles and a large, stained glass window in the chancel depicting the initiation of Christ add colour to the spartan interior of the church; *Sunday service: 0800 (Tamil) 0930 (Malayalam).*

*** Someshwara Temple (3 km) **D1 163**

This Shiva temple is one of the few monuments from the time of Kempe Gowda I which is still beautifully preserved. The

Someshwara Temple

oldest part of this Dravidian style temple is the 'garbha griha' (sanctum sanctorum) which was built during the reign of the Cholas. It was added to and further embellished by Kempe Gowda I in the sixteenth century. It is said that Kempe Gowda's interest in Shaivism was first aroused when as a captive of the Vijayanagar king he saw the fine Shiva temples at Hampi and vowed to worship Shiva if he was released.

The pillars in the mantapa (columned hall) are shaped like men on rearing horses. The pillars also contain carved figures of gods and goddesses in their various forms and mythical 'vyalis' present in every temple to ward off the evil eye. Along the outer wall of the temple are delightfully carved 'rasis' or figures representing the zodiac. On one of the walls is a figure dressed in a long gown and leaning cross-legged on a stick which is believed to be a representation of Kempe Gowda himself.

* **Bangalore Palace** (3 km) **D1 151**

The Bangalore palace is modelled on the Windsor Castle in England and is part of a vast private estate. The palace was the residence of the ex-prince Srikantadatta Wodeyar. The grounds are open to the public for marriage receptions and large public functions.

Bangalore Palace

*** Ulsoor Lake** (3 km) **C3 153, C1 163**

The Ulsoor Lake which spreads over one and a half square kilometres is a pleasant place for picnics and for boating within the city. Paddle boats, row boats and motor boats are available for hire.

From an artificial island which has large shady trees one can watch ducks or the occasional coot feeding amongst the lily leaves. A small but adequate restaurant is attached to the lake complex. Close by on the Ulsoor Rock stands one of Kempe Gowda II's four towers marking the eastern limits of his city.

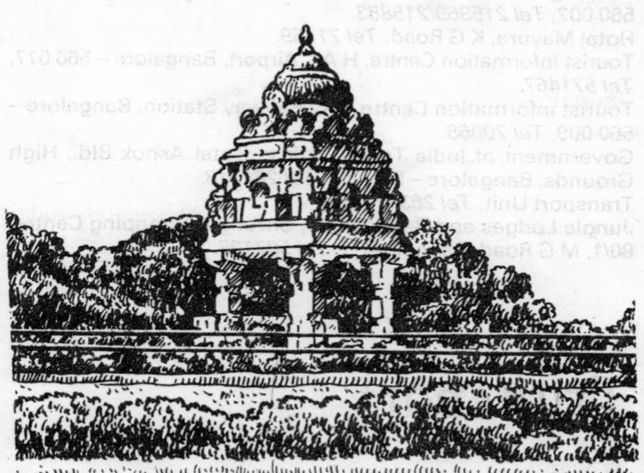

Kempe Gowda's Tower (Eastern)

Tourist Information Bureaus

Karnataka State Tourism Development Corporation (KSTDC)

KSTDC Head Office at 10/4 Kasturba Road, Bangalore – 560 001, *Tel 212901.*
Booking Counter: Badami House, N R Square, Bangalore – 560 002, *Tel 215869/215883.*
Hotel Mayura, K G Road, *Tel 71759.*
Tourist Information Centre, H A L Airport, Bangalore – 560 017, *Tel 571467.*
Tourist Information Centre, City Railway Station, Bangalore – 560 009, *Tel 70068.*
Government of India Tourist Office, Hotel Ashok Bld., High Grounds, Bangalore – 560 001, *Tel 261048.*
Transport Unit, *Tel 263113.*
Jungle Lodges and Resorts Ltd., Shrungar Shopping Centre, 80/1, M G Road, Bangalore-1, *Tel 587195.*

Transport

At first glance Bangalore may seem (like many other Indian cities) a complex maze of streets. However, it is a comparatively easy city to sightsee. There are two main arterial roads—Sankey's Road and M G–Kasturba Road. All the roads in Bangalore ultimately join these two roads. Bangalore's main modes of transport are buses and autorickshaws. However, walking through many parts of Bangalore is very enjoyable especially in the vicinity of the city market area. Taxis are considerably more expensive and not as easily available as autorickshaws though they are always available at the City Railway Station and the airport.

Bus

Bangalore has a well connected but not always punctual bus service which operates between *0600–2200* from six major bus stations: the main City Bus Station opposite the Railway Station *Tel 27090*, City Market Station *Tel 602177*, Jayanagar *Tel 64126*, Malleswaram *Tel 368697*, Shivaji Nagar *Tel 565332* and Ulsoor *Tel 571427*. A 'night special' service also operates between *2200–0600*, mainly from the City Bus Station.

Buses on major routes are frequent during rush hours. All bus stations have an information counter. The Bangalore Transport Service (BTS) also offers a 'Ladies Special' along certain routes during peak commuter hours and the faster 'Express Service' which halts at fewer bus stops.

Autorickshaw

There are about 10,000 autorickshaws plying within the city and its suburbs. They are a convenient mode of transport because they are easily available and can be manoeuvred in Bangalore's narrow lanes and crowded streets. Most auto drivers are affable and honest and are amazingly multilingual.

Besides Kannada they usually understand Hindi, Tamil and simple English. The fare charges are Rs 2.00 per km with a minimum fare of Rs 4.00 for three passengers. When operating out of city limits and between *2200* and *0500*, the autos charge one and a half times the normal meter reading.

Transport tips:

- Most autos in Bangalore have meters. When getting in, one must ensure that the meter is set at minimum fare (Rs 4.00).
- It is advisable that one mentions a prominent landmark close to one's destination like an auditorium, a cinema house, a hotel etc. if the driver seems uncertain.
- One should identify a few landmarks before one's journey which will help ensure that one is on the right course.
- One should be firm if the driver demands excess fare for reasons except those given above.
- One shouldn't hesitate to request police assistance; the constables are helpful and are ready to deal with an incalcitrant driver. At places where the drivers may be tempted to demand exhorbitant fares (e.g., railway stations, bus stations, airports) there is usually a briskly moving queue for autos super-

vised by the Bangalore police which ensures autos for everyone at normal rates. There is also a fare chart displayed at these places.

- The waiting charge usually is: first five minutes free and 50p. for every fifteen minutes or fraction thereof. But most drivers do not follow this rule and so it is better to negotiate the rates beforehand.
- One can also hire an auto for the whole day. Depending upon one's itinerary a fixed price can be negotiated which usually works out to about Rs 120 a day.
- Auto stands are located all over the city at convenient spots.

Car hire

Chauffeur driven ordinary and airconditioned cars, though expensive, are a reasonable proposition if four or five people are travelling together. This is true especially of trips to nearby tourist spots outside Bangalore (see Places of Interest Outside Bangalore). For larger parties, vans and mini-buses are also available. Many of the larger hotels in the city have their own car/van hiring service and almost all hotels have a travel agency located in the premises which will make the necessary arrangements. The Karnataka State Tourism Development Corporation (KSTDC), India Tourism Development Corporation (ITDC) as well as several other approved tourist car operators all over the city (listed in the Directory) also offer cars and vans on hire.

Conducted Tours

The KSTDC and several other agencies listed in the Directory offer guided sightseeing tours of Bangalore and outstation tourist spots. For those who prefer a more leisurely pace for their sightseeing, guides speaking English, Hindi and certain foreign languages can be hired through the Government of India Tourist Office, Hotel Ashoka Bldg., *Tel 261048*, Dept. of Tourism, Government of Karnataka, Kaveri Bhavan, *Tel 211186*. Rates are fixed by the tourist offices; boarding and lodging of the guide in the case of an overnight stay and a lunch allowance in the case of day trips are extra and are also fixed by the government. Not all guided tours include extras such as entry fee to monuments and museums and meals in their fare charge. It is better to check what one is entitled to when one buys the ticket.

KSTDC Tours

Bangalore City Tour (1/2 day)

Morning: *(daily 0730–1330)* Tipu Sultan's palace, Bull Temple, Lal Bagh, Commercial Street and M G Road, Visvesvaraya Technological Museum, Government Museum and Venkatappa Art Gallery, Vidhana Soudha, Government Soap Factory and Anjaneya Swamy Temple.

Trips begin at Badami House, N R Square, opposite the City Corporation Office and terminate at the City Railway Station.

Evening: *(daily 1330–1930)* Vidhana Soudha, Visvesvaraya Technological Museum, Government Museum, Venkatappa Art Gallery, Tipu Sultan's Palace, Bull Temple, Anjaneya Temple, Lal Bagh, Ulsoor Lake, Commercial Street and M G Road. Trips begin and end at the City Railway Station.

Out of Bangalore Tours

Mysore *(daily 0715–2230)* Shrirangapattana (Daria Daulat, Gumbaz, Ranganathaswamy Temple), St Philomena's Church, Cauvery Arts and Crafts Emporium, Chamundi Hills, Mysore Zoo, Mysore Palace, Jagan Mohan Art Gallery, Brindavan Gardens.

Shravanabelagola–Belur–Halebid *(daily 0715–2230)* Jain pilgrimage centre of Shravanabelagola, Hoysala temples of Chenna Keshava at Belur and Hoysaleshwara at Halebid.

Mantralaya–Tungabhadra Dam–Hampi *(Fri dep. 2200–Sun arr. 2200)* Mantralaya, Tungabhadra River Dam and the famous Vijayanagar capital of Hampi. Fare inclusive of accommodation.

Temple Tour *(daily 2230–0800 3rd day)* Tirupati, Tirumala, Mangapura, Kalahasthi. Fare inclusive of special darshan at Tirupati and accommodation.

Ooty *(daily during season, Mon and Fri off season. 0715–2230 3rd day)* Shrirangapattana (Ranganathaswamy

Temple, Gumbaz, Daria Daulat), St Philomena's Church, Chamundi Hills, Mysore Zoo, Palace, Jagan Mohan Art Gallery, Brindavan Gardens, Ooty (Botanical Gardens, Ooty Lake, Commercial Street), Coonoor sightseeing.

Reservations: KSTDC Information Counter, Badami House, N R Square, Opposite City Corporation Office; *Tel 222541*. KSTDC Head Office, 10/4 Kasturba Road; *Tel 212901*.
Also from KSTDC information Counters at the airport; *Tel 571467* and City Railway Station, *Tel 70068* as well as authorised selling agents and travel agencies.
Tours start and terminate at Badami House, N R Square, *Tel 215869/215883* unless otherwise mentioned.

Museums and Libraries

Bangalore's three museums (Government Museum, Venkatappa Art Gallery and Visvesvaraya Technological Museum) are conveniently located next to each other on Kasturba Road, but are closed on different days.
Government Museum: *open 1000–1700; closed Wed; Tel 564483.*
Venkatappa Art Gallery: *open 1000–1700; closed Wed; Tel 564483.*
Visvesvaraya Technological Museum: *open 1000–1700; closed Mon; Tel 544076.*

Although there are only three museums there are many libraries in the city. Most social and cultural organisations usually have a corpus of books and periodicals which are accessible to the public, sometimes with special permission. There are also reference libraries attached to educational and training institutions which are usually available to scholars and researchers.

Tamil Sangam 29/1, Annaswamy Mudaliar Road, *Tel 570062.* **C1 163**

This association caters to the large Tamil population in Bangalore and has a well stocked library on Tamil literature. It also conducts courses in Tamil and Kannada and holds classes in yoga, tailoring, handicrafts, music and dance.

Bharatiya Vidya Bhavan Race Course Road, *Tel 267421.*

The Bangalore wing of this nationwide organisation is actively engaged in literary, educational and cultural activities. The extensive library contains books on fiction and non-fiction and is open to members only. Membership can be acquired on payment of a nominal fee. **C3 151**

Gokhale Institute of Public Affairs Narasimharaja Colony, Bangalore-19, *Tel 602436.* **B2 168**

This institution established in 1945 is named after the lawyer and freedom fighter Gopalkrishna Gokhale and endeavours to build an awareness of democratic citizenship in the public. Views on current affairs expressed during discussions organised by the Institute are passed on to the concerned government authority. The library contains books on law, the Constitution, economics and philosophy. There is a large section devoted to fiction which is of special interest to those interested in old, out of print books.

Indian Institute of World Culture 6, B P Wadia Road, Basavangudi, *Tel 602581.* **C2 169**

The aim of this nonsectarian institution is to promote the spirit of brotherhood among people of all communities and nationalities. Meetings are held every week. The library has back issues of national and international journals, a wide range of fiction and a fine collection of books on philosophy.

British Library 29, St Mark's Road, *Tel 213485.* **A1 162**

Started in 1960 the library possesses a collection of some 30,000 books and 80 magazines published in the UK mainly dealing with subjects like medicine, applied sciences and technical literature. There is also a small section on fiction. Besides, the library provides microfilm, video and audio cassettes for educational purposes. It also offers photocopying facilities. The library is for use by members only. **A1 160**

Sri Ramakrishna Math Library Bull Temple Road, Basavangudi, *Tel 602681.* **B1 168**

Attached to the Sri Ramakrishna Math which was founded in 1904 the library has an authoritative collection of books on the Hindu religion, mythology and philosophy in Kannada, English and other regional languages; *open 0900–1100; 1600–1900.*

Indo-German Cultural Society (Max Mueller Bhavan), 3, Lavelle Road, Bangalore-1, *Tel 215435* **B2 162**

In keeping with its objectives of fostering cultural relations between India and Germany, the library contains books and journals on Germany and a large collection of German literary works.

Alliance Francaise de Bangalore, 16, N & G M T Road, near Cantonment Railway Station, *Tel 278762.*

Besides conducting courses in French and organising film shows, exhibitions and cultural activities, the AF also lends out films. The library contains a variety of books and magazines on France and a comprehensive section on French fiction. **B1 162**

Mythic Society, Nrupathunga Road, *Tel 215034.*

This voluntary public organisation has a library which is invaluable for students of Indology. It contains over 10,000 volumes on anthropology, epigraphy, numismatics, ethnology, mythology and folklore, linguistics, etc.

Other libraries which can be used for reference are:

The Gandhi Sahitya Sangha, 8th Cross, Malleswaram, *Tel 365186.*

The Theosophical Society, 'Maitri Bhavan', 90 K R Road, Basavangudi, *Tel 605440.*

Karnataka Sahitya Academy Library, 14/3 Nrupathunga Rd, *Tel 211730.*

Urdu Library Centre, 37 City Market, *Tel 76151.*

Libraries which can be used for reference with special permission are:
Government Secretariat Library, Vidhana Soudha. Contact Director, Karnataka State Archives. *Tel 264465.*
Lalit Kala Academy Library, *Tel 215297*, for reference books on painting, sculpture, graphics, etc.
Indian Institute of Science Library, *Tel 344411.*
Karnataka Janapada Trust Museum, Kumara Park West, for information on folklore of Karnataka, *Tel 362768.*

Sports and Hobbies

Bangalore's pleasant climate makes it a suitable place for a variety of outdoor sport. Cricket is by far the most popular game. Bangalore has many parks and gardens which provide excellent pitches for an impromptu game of cricket. Enthusiastic crowds converge around the Bangalore Turf Club during season time; *open summer: mid-May – end July; winter: November – March.*

Swimming is also a popular pastime. The corporation has provided seven swimming pools in the city. Many hotels, clubs and institutes also provide this facility for their clients and members. Some of them offer golf, tennis, flying, riding, and yoga as well.

To avail of these facilities it is necessary to become a member of the clubs that offer them. A visitor may be granted a temporary membership to these clubs when his name is proposed by a permanent member. Sometimes the club facilities can be used if the visitor is a guest of a member. Many hotels offer annual memberships for the use of their swimming pools and health clubs; single visits are also allowed on payment of a fee. Flower shows and dog shows are also popular occasions.

Bangalore also offers a fairly active night-life; walking along M G Road and Brigade Road and peering into the brightly lit, attractively displayed shop-windows can be a pleasant experience.

Basketball: Karnataka State Basketball Association, 14/3, 10th 'c' Main Road, Jayanagar, *Tel 606902.*
Billiards: Karnataka State Billiards Association, 5 Miller Tank Bund Area, Vasanthanagar, *Tel 200432/200419.*
Boating: Hessaraghatta Boating Club, Hesaraghatta & Ulsoor Lake. (Row boats and motor boats on hire.)
Cricket: Karnataka State Cricket Association, M G Road, *Tel 564578/564487.*
Flying: Jakkur Flying Club, Jakkur.
Golf: Bangalore Golf Club, High Grounds, *Tel 200312/266713/267121.*
Riding: The B.A.R.I., c/o The Turf Club, Race Course Road, *Tel 264944.*
Racing: Bangalore Turf Club, Race Course Road, *Tel 262391.*
Swimming: Although most hotels allow the use of the pool to everybody subject to the payment of a fee, some reserve the pool for residents only.
Hotels:
Hotel Ashok, High Grounds; *Tel 269462.*
Hotel Harsha, Tasker Town; *Tel 565566.*
West End Hotel, Race Course Road, *Tel 269281/264191.*
Windsor Manor, 25, Sankey Road, *Tel 269898.*
B.D.A. Swimming Pool, III Block Jayanagar. Admission fee Re 2.50 per person per hour; *open 0630–0930; 1600–1800; Sun 0900–1300; 1400–1700; closed Thurs.*
Bangalore Club, 225, Field Marshal Cariappa Road, *Tel 211374/211416.*
Corporation Swimming Pools; Kensington Park, Ulsoor.
Corporation Office Compound, Sri Narasimharaja Circle, *Tel 238540.*
Mahalakshmi Layout, Rajajinagar.
Sankey Road Swimming Pool, Bhasyam Circle, Sadashivanagar.
Seshadripuram, Nehrunagar.
Kempambudi Tank, Gavipuram.
The corporation pools charge very nominal entrance fees. They do however, have separate timings for men and women.
Tennis: All India Lawn Tennis Association, 289, 10th Main Road, 3rd Block, Jayanagar, *Tel 601126.*
Bangalore Tennis Club, 168, 3rd Cross Domlur, 2nd stage-38, *Tel 564358.*
Yoga: Arogya Yogasana Shala, 10/8th Main, Sadashiva Nagar, *Tel 345100.*
Tamil Sangam, 29/1 Annaswamy Mudaliar Road, *Tel 570062.*
International Yoga Institute, Bank of India, K G Road, *Tel 29477.*
Institute of Naturopathy and Yogic Sciences, 16 Tumkur Road, (opp. Jindal Factory), *Tel 396339/396337.*
Atma Darshan Yogashram, 213, 30th cross, 7th Block, Jayanagar, *Tel 647839.*

Sadhana Sangama Trust (R), 635, 10th Cross West of Chord Road, 2nd Stage Mahalakshmi Layout, Bangalore-86, *Tel 323898.*
Sri Surya Prakash Institute of Yoga for Women, 115/1, Nehru Circle, Seshadripuram, *Tel 369382.*

Shopping

Shopping in Bangalore is an exciting activity. Shops cater to the tastes of every kind of shopper. Goods range from the latest in sophisticated electronic goods at prices that are among the lowest in India to textiles of traditional hue and weave, and finely crafted woodwork and pottery. Service in most shops is good; salespersons are genuinely eager to please with the result that shoppers happily buy everything that they can. Silks and handloom fabrics, readymade garments, woollen carpets, cotton and woollen dhurries, sandalwood articles, teak and rosewood carvings with ivory inlay work, furniture, electronic items, gold and silver jewellery and of course agarbathis and 'attars' are considered good buys in Bangalore.

Most shops are open Monday through Saturday from *1000–2000* with a lunch break of about two hours from *1300–1500.* It is possible to get a lower price for one's purchases by bargaining. In most smaller shops one can actively bargain for 10–20 per cent lower than the prices quoted, and it is not unusual to ask for discounts in larger establishments if one has bought several items from the same place or an item of considerable value. This is not possible in government emporia. Shops announce discount sales for all festive occasions, especially for Ugadi, the Ganesha festival, Dussehra, Deepavali and Christmas.

Prices often vary from shop to shop, so if one finds that something is too expensive at a given place one must be sure to check prices in other shops as well.

Most shops accept credit cards. Large established shops and government emporia will accept foreign credit cards too. However, the smaller shops insist on cash sales.

Textiles and Handicrafts

Bangalore silk saris, a light printed silk variety, is very attractive and is reasonably priced. The silk is woven in various towns around the city, notably Channapattana, 59 km away, which is also famous for its spun silk. It is also woven in Bangalore city in the small houses of Cubbon pete. The busy clack and hum of the powerlooms in each house is a prevailing feature of this locality. Mysore silk, heavier and often with borders of glittering zari, are also easily available. Crepe silk, soft silk and silk georgette are the three varieties available in Mysore silk which is priced according to the weight of the silk and the quantity of zari it contains.

Other silk varieties are: Monakalmur silk, Doddaballapur silk, Dharmavaram, Kanchipuram and other varieties from Tamil Nadu, and an extensive range of north Indian saris.

Cotton saris are not as popular but Mettur and Davangere cotton saris are available as also other cotton varieties from Tamil Nadu and other parts of India.

The Regional Design Centre at Sagar complex on Kempe Gowda Road is actively engaged in experiments with different fabrics and designs for saris. The centre also gives expert advice on weaving and dyeing methods. One can also get information on handloom silk from here.

Best shops: Cauvery Emporium (M G Road), Vijayalakshmi (M G Road), Deepam Silks (M G Road), Janardhan (Unity Building, J C Road), Vimor (Victoria Layout; run by Mrs. Nanjappa, for exclusive printed and heavy silks), Pallavi (Double Road, for cottons), Vedanta (Safina Plaza for cottons), the KSIC Showroom (M G Road), Handloom House (M G Road), Cottage Industries Emporium (M G Road), Nataraj Silk House (206, Chikpet), Sudarshan Silks and Saris (231, Krishna Market, Chikpet), Mysore Silk Emporium (47, B V K Iyengar Road), Mysore Handicrafts Emporium (Commercial Street). Note: Prices in Commercial Street tend to be higher than in other parts of the city.

There are many boutiques, often in private homes, which advertise only occasionally in the papers. One should keep an eye out for signboards when one goes around the city.

Bangalore is famous for its brass and lacquerware, wood carving in teak and rosewood, ivory and sandalwood articles, and attractively designed pottery. The Regional Design Centre on Church Street creates unusual and attractive items in wood, stone, brass and potteryware using a synthesis of local craft and modern designs.

Attractive pottery and terracotta items are available at Cauvery Emporium; ceramics, glassware, pot hangers, cane baskets and table mats at Collections (St Patrick's Complex on Brigade Road); table linen, furniture, etchings, lampshades etc. and Auroville products at Art Works (Brigade Road); handmade paper, artefacts, silk scarves, perfumes, soaps, agarbathis, bathsalts, etc. at Ship (Church Street).

Best Shops: Cottage Industries Emporium (M G Road), Cauvery Emporium (M G Road), Natesans (M G Road); for antiques, Rugs and Riches (M G Road); for curios, Heirlooms (M G Road).

Other Shopping Areas

Bangalore also offers a variety of footwear. Famous shoe shops like Metro stock the latest in shoes and are expensive. Shops on Commercial Street and Old Poorhouse Road are ideal for a more economical range of shoes. Lidkar's, a Government of Karnataka undertaking, provides quality leather shoes and other goods like wallets and purses and snakeskin articles at reasonable rates. Hi-design stocks well-finished cow-hide goods like travelling bags, handbags, chairs, etc.

'Appalams' and 'vadaams' (ready-to-fry crunchy eatables), ready-to-mix powders for various delicious south Indian dishes, pickles and the famous south Indian coffee powder can be bought from Mavalli Tiffin Rooms (MTR), tiny shops in the City Market area, and the Nilgiris Dairy (Brigade Road) which is also a good place to buy milk, cheese, ghee, bread, tinned foods, toiletries, cereals (whole and ground), essences, etc; the Supermarket on Brigade Road opposite Nilgiris Dairy also sells an amazing range of foods like Ooty cheese, etc. Nayak's (Margosa Road, near 11th cross, Malleswaram) sells high quality appalams and powdered spices; India Coffee Depot (21 Museum Road, 36 Sampige Road, 38 Prithvi Buildings, K G Road) sells excellent coffee powder.

Books: Premier Book shop (Church Street), Gangarams, Higginbothams (M G Road), Orient Longman (M G Road), Macmillan and Oxford University Press (along M G Road); Select Book Shop (35/1 Brigade Road Cross) for out of print and rare books and periodicals—a real treasure-house for booklovers. Occasionally it has old prints and etchings for sale.

Richard Square (near Russel Market) for cutlery, crockery and household items.
Commercial Street for hosiery, textiles, woollen materials, furnishings, travelling goods, sarees, jewellery and general merchandise.
Residency Road for steel furniture and a number of state emporia (Gangotri, Mrignayani, Gurjari) for handicrafts in metal, clay and wood.
Chickpet for silk saris, silver and gold jewellery and textiles.
Arcot Srinivasachari Street for metal items, brass, aluminium and copperware.
B.V.K. Iyengar Road for wood products, plywood, paper and electrical goods.

Avenue Road for stationery, stainless steel wares and silver jewellery.
Kasturba Gandhi Road (K G Road) for textiles and saris.
Jayachamaraja Road (JC Road) for automobile parts.
Sri Narasimharaja Road (SNR Road) for sanitary ware, chemicals and dyes, hardware, and steel and wooden furniture.

Recreation

Music and Dance

The cultural scene in Bangalore is vibrant and diverse. Bangalore's mixed ethnic population is reflected in its music concerts, dance performances and plays which are staged frequently. Performances of Hindustani (north Indian classical) music and various north Indian dance forms like Kathak and Odissi are as well attended as concerts of Carnatic (south Indian classical) music and dance forms like Bharatha Natyam, Kuchipudi and Kathakali. Western and fusion-style musicians also love to play to Bangalore's enthusiastic audiences.

There are several art and dance forms indigenous to Karnataka and the chief amongst them is the 'Yakshagana', a folk dance which originates from coastal Karnataka. The Yakshagana requires elaborate makeup and costumes and is in this way similar to Kathakali. This dance form also involves a lot of commentary and was originally intended for the entertainment of village folk on festive and religious occasions. The Yakshagana was held in the open air on a stage illuminated with oil lamps. It began late at night and continued till dawn. The purpose of the Yakshagana was to impart knowledge and values to the villagers by enacting stories from the Puranas and the two great epics the *Ramayana* and the *Mahabharatha*. Today the Yakshagana can be enjoyed in the comfort of modern auditoria.

The two main music seasons in Bangalore are in April–May during the Ramnavami festival and in September–October during the Dussehra festival. During these two seasons the music activities are at their peak. While some cultural associations, especially those in Seshadripuram and Chamarajapet, are famous for their rich musical fare several smaller community organisations also offer their own programmes in halls and auditoria all over the city.

Yakshagana

Every year the Society for Promotion of Indian Classical Music and Culture Among Youth (Spic-Macay) organises free concerts in various parts of the city. The festival is usually held in January and February and gives the people of Bangalore a chance to enjoy the performances of famous singers, dancers and musicians from all over the country.

Details of forthcoming music and art festivals are given sufficiently in advance in the daily newspapers and also in the lively weekly 'Sunday Mid-Day'. Moderately priced tickets are available at the venues.

Bharatha Natyam and Carnatic music are very popular here. Bangalore has hundreds of little schools run by community associations or eminent dancers and musicians, scattered all over the city, which teach these forms of music and dance.

Saraswathi Sangeetha Vidyalaya, 114 Nehru Circle, *Tel 363900*.
Tarangini Institute of Veena, Sirur Park, Malleswaram, *Tel 361906*.
Keshava Nruthya Sala, 2nd Stage Rajaji Nagar, *Tel 320903*.

Geetha Mandira Music and Dance School, 389, 9th Main Road, Hanumanthanagara.
Gandharva Nruthyashala, Kumara Park (w).
Usha Datar, 29, 13k, 1st Block, 14th Cross, 19th B Main, Rajajinagar. (For Kathak)
Prof. U S Krishnarao, 7/2 A Palace Cross, *Tel 363298.*
Nruthya Vidya Niketana, II Main, Chamarajapet.
Veena Vishalakshmi Kala Kendra, 108/A, R M Vilas Extn.
Vijaya College of Music, 4th Block Jayanagar, *Tel 641896.*

Art Schools
Chitra Kala Parishad, Kumara High Grounds, *Tel 71816.*
Ken School of Arts, Seshadripuram.
Mangala Kala Niketan, No. 12, 14th A Cross, 11th Main Road, Malleswaram.
Kala Mandir School of Art, Basavangudi.

Auditoria

Ravindra Kalakshetra, *Tel 221271.*
Town Hall, *Tel 221270.*
Bal Bhavan, *Tel 564189.*
Visvesvaraya Industrial Museum Hall, *Tel 544076.*
Chowdiah Memorial Hall, *Tel 365810.*
Bangalore Gayana Samaja, *Tel 606049.*
Institution of Engineers, *Tel 264698.*
Guru Nanak Bhavan, *Tel 260198.*
Yavanika Auditorium, Nrupathunga Road.
Bharatiya Vidya Bhavan, *Tel 267421.*
Kannada Sahitya Parishad, *Tel 602991.*

Watching films is a favourite pastime for many Bangaloreans. Several films in various Indian languages are made in Bangalore every year. Although social comedies for the whole family are preferred, some recent attempts to make films with social and political themes have been widely acclaimed. Film studios allow one to watch film makers at work, but a prior appointment is needed.

Chamundeshwar Studio and Lab, 48, Millers Tank Bund Road, *Tel 268642*.
Shree Kanteerava Studio Ltd., Tumkur Road, Yeshwantpur, *Tel 368611*.

Theatre

Kannada theatre is extremely popular in Bangalore and consists mainly of political satire and light comedies. Plays are mostly organised by community associations but there are also some amateur groups like the Yashasvi Theatre Group ('yashasvi' means success) which stages plays in Kannada. The Theatre Arts Group, Play Pen, The Bangalore Little Theatre and other groups regularly stage plays in English. Drama companies touring India under the auspicies of the British Council and Max Mueller Bhavan also stage performances in the city from time to time. Details of plays appear in newspapers.

Eating Out

For residents who like an occasional change from eating at home and for the tourist who enjoys good food, Bangalore offers excellent culinary fare. The hospitable foodloving native Kannadigas and the cosmopolitan population which later settled in the city have ensured that a wide range of eateries offering a variety of cuisines is available—Chinese, north Indian, Continental and south Indian.

Some of the well known restaurants are listed in the Directory with an index indicating the type of food they offer and the price range for an average meal (without liquor), for one person. In establishments where service charge is not included, tips of upto ten per cent of the bill are expected.

Unlike north Indian food, south Indian cuisine depends heavily upon rice which is eaten with an astonishing range of 'dhals' (lentils) and vegetables delightfully different in taste from anything offered in north India. The ubiquitious 'meals' offered in roadside cafés and posh restaurants are moderately priced, filling and provide a very interesting introduction to the gastronomic delights of south India. A waiter bearing a large bowl of rice will pile the 'thali' (or banana leaf) with hot steaming rice, followed by another who will generously ladle warm ghee (clarified butter) on to it. In the meantime a variety of dishes will be served—little bowls containing sambar (spiced lentils), rasam (the famous peppery spiced watery soup, either eaten with rice or drunk as a digestive at the end of the meal), vegetables, yogurt and usually a sweet. There are regional variations in the preparations of this basic meal. Kannadiga food is neither too hot nor too bland. One of its specialities is 'bisi bele hulianna', a delicious spicy dish made with rice, vegetables and lentils cooked together. Another south Indian meal which is relatively unknown in the north is 'tiffin', a catchword for all snacks such as 'idli' (soft, steamed, rice cakes), 'dosai' (crisp pancakes made from a rice and lentil batter) eaten plain or stuffed (masala dosai) and vadai (lentil dumplings, crisp outside and soft inside), all of which can be eaten as breakfast, at teatime or as anytime snacks. A delicious 'tiffin' unique to Bangalore is the 'chow-chow bath' (two steaming, hot ladles of a savoury 'kara bath' and a sweet 'kesari bath', both of semolina.

Bangalore is also the home for the *Mavalli Tiffin Rooms* (MTR) famous for their Udipi dishes (cooks from Udipi, a small town in Karnataka, are reputed to be very good). Although there are many other restaurants now that serve Udipi food (the *Kamat Hotel* chain is another well known one) the MTR has been around for years and has established a name for itself for the quality of its food and is now as synonymous with Bangalore as the Lal Bagh next to which it is situated. Its popularity draws crowds of food lovers. To ensure that one gets a seat it would be wise to go there at least half an hour before they open in the morning *0630–1100* and in the afternoon *1530–1730*. The eminently readable injunctions festooned all over the restaurant on how to conduct oneself while in the restaurant are almost as famous as the food offered there! If one cannot manage a visit to the restaurant, however, one could always rustle up some MTR magic at home—their ready-to-make mixes are as delicious as the original!

There is a large concentration of restaurants and pubs around the M G Road, Brigade Road and Church Street areas. These usually serve Chinese, north Indian and Continental dishes, fast food and drinks.

For those visitors with a sweet tooth Bangalore has a host of pastry shops and ice cream parlours. The *Sweet Chariot* on

Brigade Road sells excellent cakes and pastries while the *Lakeview* ice cream parlour on M G Road is famous for its special 'Black Widow'. Intoxicatingly good rum tarts and other pastries are sold at *Melting Moments* on M G Road. The *Indiana* ice cream parlour on Residency Road hands out freshly made ice creams with some unusual flavours. *K C Das* on St Mark's Road has very good Bengali sweets and also superb sweet curd served in earthenware cups which impart a special flavour to it. *Bhagat Rams* on Commercial Street sells great 'jalebis', 'gulab jamuns' and other freshly made sweets. Their savoury samosas are excellent.

Another famous eating area is in the vicinity of the City Market and K G Road, one of the oldest parts of the city. Here tiny restaurants several decades old with tiled walls and marble topped tables jostle with larger commercial establishments. Most of these eateries serve vegetarian Udipi food and are extremely cheap; one can get a masala dosai, 'tayir vadai' (lentil dumplings soaked in curd) and a glass of coffee for about Rs 12. Many of these restaurants cheerfully let two people share a coffee. Some restaurants do not allow this and so the rather confusing notice 'No by two service' and sometimes funnier versions of the same warning are displayed prominently on the walls.

The city has a flourishing Muslim population so there are a variety of restaurants which dish up universal non-vegetarian delights. Mutton and chicken biryani, kababs and large chewy tandoory rotis are available at unbelievably low rates.

In Chickpet are also found long established sweet shops known for their quality products. *Arya Bhavan Sweets* in Kempe Gowda Circle with a branch at Balepet is one such institution specialising in a delicious light concoction called 'son papri'. *Sri Venkateshwara Sweetmeat Stall* at Balepet is worth a visit for its 'badam halwa' and certain Kannadiga specialities like 'chandrakala,' 'kalakandh' and 'chiroti'. *Sri Ramavilas* on Gundopanth Street serves crumbly 'Mysore pak' and 'dumrote', a chewy sweet made of pumpkin. However, it would be wise to drink a little ginger juice with salt or 'jal jeera' (water mixed with powdered cummin seed) before indulging in these sweet delights. Both are excellent digestives.

Five star hotels feature at least one restaurant. They are considerably more expensive, usually averaging to above Rs 75 per person per meal. Pleasing decor, soft piped music or in some cases live bands, and quick and courteous service are the hallmark of these places though in many cases the food is not always upto the expected standard.

While many visitors feel that the city is a culinary delight, Bangalore's pubs are another major attraction. Immensely popular with citizens and visitors alike, the 100 odd pubs scattered around the city offer draught beer in a friendly, comfortable atmosphere. Several restaurants in the city also have bars attached.

Accommodation

Most of Bangalore's hotels and lodges are located around Sankey's Road and M G Road/Kasturba Road where restaurants, shops and modes of transport are within easy reach. They vary from the luxurious five star hotels which offer services and facilities like room service, beauty parlours and swimming pools to the more moderately priced hotels. Sometimes, one may find them classified under the heads 'Western' and 'Indian' the difference being that western style hotels are more decor conscious, almost always airconditioned and consequently more expensive. 'Indian' style hotels have considerably fewer frills, the rooms are clean but modestly furnished and the tariff is usually much lower. In a few cases the 'Indian' prefix refers to the toilet. ('Western' hotels invariably have the western style wc.)

Bangalore has a large number of budget hotels (about Rs 75 and Rs 150 for single and double rooms) and moderate hotels (between Rs 150 and Rs 300 for single and double rooms). The moderate hotels often offer a choice of rooms airconditioned and non-airconditioned. A room which is not airconditioned would cost about 30–50 per cent less than an airconditioned one. Moderate hotels usually have a vegetarian restaurant attached. They also offer amenities like room service and trunk call bookings.

The services and facilities offered in the budget category hotels may vary, sometimes quite sharply. Generally in places which charge less than Rs 150 for a double room one can expect a clean albeit bare room with a ceiling fan (and perhaps even a mosquito net!) with an attached bath (in some hotels one may have to share a bathroom). Guests in many of these budget hotels are treated to a quaint form of room service. The 'room boys' cheerfully take care of every need, be it serving the morning coffee, getting shoes polished and clothes laundered, or even summoning a barber for a quick shave or haircut! Tips of a rupee or more for each service performed ensures prompt attendance for the duration of the stay.

In five star hotels a tip for the room service staff and the bell boy is expected but not necessary. In the restaurants of these hotels a tip of about 10 per cent of the bill is usually given.

Most hotels insist on a *1200* check in/out although the hotels in the budget category are more flexible about this rule. Most hotels will on request install an extra bed to accommodate an extra person. The additional charge usually works out to about 25–50 per cent above the normal tariff. Most hotels also include a service charge, sales tax, and in the case of the five star hotels luxury tax as well.

Railway passengers can use the comfortable railway retiring rooms at the Bangalore City Railway Station for a period of upto 72 hours from the time of checking in. These are particularly useful if one arrives at Bangalore late at night or does not intend to spend more than a couple of days in the city. The double rooms with an attached bath (clean linen is also provided) cost Rs 50 a day. Special rooms for three people at Rs 75 a day are available and an extra bed for a fourth member can be arranged for Rs 7 a day. Special permission from the Station Superintendent is needed if one wants to use the room for more than 72 hours.

Religious institutions, choultries (rest houses) and dharmashalas also provide accommodation either in rooms or dormitories with shared bathrooms.

The centrally located YMCA on Nrupathunga Road, *Tel 211848,* offers double and single rooms with a common bath for Rs 50 and double rooms with attached bath for Rs 100 for a short period, on a night to night basis. Unfortunately it is restricted to men only. The YWCA guest house on Infantry Road, *Tel 570997,* is open only to women. The Youth Hostels Association of India allows one to stay for a maximum of five days at nominal rates but is restricted to their members. For large groups, marriage halls called kalyana mantaps which have rooms with bath and cooking facilities are available. (The rates are subject to change from time to time).

Annual Events

JANUARY

Flower Show: The first of the famous biannual flower and fruit shows is held in Lal Bagh's glass house by the Mysore Horticultural Society in January. This show attracts many competitors and prizes are awarded to the best exhibits. There is a brisk sale of seeds and saplings in the numerous stalls that line the sides of the glass house.

Republic Day (26) : This national holiday is celebrated with flag hoisting ceremonies and parades in schools, colleges and government institutions. A grand parade in the Kanteerava Stadium close to the City Corporation is the highlight of this day. Government museums and libraries remain closed on this day.

APRIL

Ugadi : This is New Year's day for some Hindus of south India. It is celebrated by wearing new clothes, visiting friends and relatives, and sharing food and sweets specially made for the festival. Discount sales offered by sari shops, furnishing shops and hardware stores during this period are eagerly awaited.

Karaga : A festival unique to Bangalore, it is celebrated by the Tigalas, a community of Tamil origin. This festival recreates the battle of Kurukshetra (in the epic *Mahabharata*). A procession of people starts from the Dharmaraja Temple on Veera Pillai Street and winds its way through the streets of old Bangalore. Fire-walking, spectacular sword play and the resonant tolling of the temple bells on a full moon night make it a magnificent spectacle.

Someshwar Car Festival (at Ulsoor): The 'utsava murthi' (idol) of this ancient temple at Ulsoor is taken out in a procession. The rituals are undertaken mainly by the Vokkalingas (a farming community) who come into the city from the rural areas.

Sri Ramanavami Festival : This festival celebrates the birth of Lord Rama. It is conducted with traditional pomp and ceremony. Music festivals lasting for about a month are organised by music associations in Sheshadripuram and Chamarajapet. Their aim is to promote and encourage Carnatic music.

MAY

Bangalore Races : The races are an important racing meet in south India. Bangalore actually has two racing seasons: *summer: (mid-May–July) and winter: (November – March).* The Race Club also has facilities for off-course betting on races in other parts of the country. This race course is one of the finest in the country.

JUNE

Id-ul-Fitr : For Muslims their month of fasting during Ramadan comes to an end when the new moon is sighted. People wear new clothes, prepare feasts and share them with the needy, and offer prayers at mosques.
(Year to year the dates of Muslim festivals change)

AUGUST

Independence Day (15) : This national holiday is celebrated with flag hoisting ceremonies and parades. The official ceremony is held at the Brigade Parade ground near Mahatma Gandhi Road.

AUGUST/SEPTEMBER

Sri Ganesha Festival : Towards the end of August

thousands of people install idols of Ganesha, the elephant-headed God of Wisdom and Learning, in their homes. Children go round the neighbourhood in an attempt to see 101 Ganeshas before the images are carried away to be immersed in Bangalore's tanks and lakes. This popular festival which lasts for about a week is enthusiastically celebrated all over Karnataka. In Bangalore music and dance programmes, fairs and exhibitions are organised for the public.

SEPTEMBER

St Mary's Feast (8) : The venerable St Mary's Bascilica celebrates its Parish Feast and the procession and ceremonies attract crowds of people from all faiths.

SEPTEMBER/OCTOBER

Dussehra : This ten day festival celebrating the battle and the ultimate victory of Goddess Chamundi over the demon Mahishasura is accompanied by community gatherings, feasting and programmes of music and dance.

OCTOBER/NOVEMBER

Deepavali : During this important festival of lights, tiny lamps are placed along window ledges and outside doors to invite Lakshmi, the Goddess of Wealth into homes. Sweets are prepared and distributed, new clothes are worn and at night everyone enthusiastically lights fireworks and bursts crackers.

NOVEMBER

Kannada Rajyotsava (1) : It celebrates the anniversary of the formation of the State of Karnataka in 1956. Cultural programmes as well as lectures and seminars are organised on this day.

NOVEMBER/DECEMBER

A groundnut fair outside the Bull Temple is held during this time of the year. After the harvest the first groundnuts of the crop are offered by the farmers to the bull.

DECEMBER

Christmas (25) : is celebrated with traditional éclat;

shopwindows particularly in the M G Road/Brigade Road/ Commercial Street area are gaily decorated. Carol services and concerts are organised by various Christian associations.

Travel

Road, rail and air links connect Bangalore to all parts of India. In some cases all three modes of transport offer at least two alternative routes, one usually being more circuitous and time consuming than the other. Tourist offices of various states and many travel agencies help to plan an itinerary within any specified time-frame. Except for road transport (where one usually needs to book only two or three days in advance) it is essential to buy the ticket as much in advance as possible. This is especially true during the holiday seasons (May-July, Dec-Jan) and during the Dussehra festival (Oct-Nov). Enquiry counters at the airport and railway stations announce arrival and departure timings (airport *Tel 142*) (City Station: *Tel 133 or 134*, Bangalore Cant. *Tel 135*). Air and rail terminals have tourist information counters and telephone facilities. Asking a travel agent to book tickets (air and rail) saves a lot of time and bother.

AIR

The state-owned Indian Airlines Corporation (IAC) is one of the largest domestic carriers in Asia connecting over eighty cities in India and the neighbouring countries. Air fares are expensive by Indian standards but this in no way affects the heavy traffic. A student concession of 25 per cent of the regular fare is available to those with proper student identification. Infants below the age of two years can travel at 10 per cent of the fare and children under 12 years can travel at 50 per cent of the total fare. Concession is also available for groups.

Indian Airlines offers 'Youth Fares' to foreigners and non-resident Indians between the ages of 12 and 30 which works out to a 25 per cent concession to be paid in foreign currency. Foreigners and non-resident Indians are also offered the 21 day 'Discover India' fare and the shorter 14 day 'Tour India' fare (to be paid in foreign currency only) which covers unlimited travel on all domestic sectors with one stop over at each point. A trip between Sri Lanka or Male and Bangalore, Coimbatore, Cochin, Trivandrum, Madurai, Tiruchirapalli and Madras can be availed of at a 30 per cent discount under the 'South Indian Excursion Fare Plan'. (For concessional tariff contact: *Tel 141.*)

Indian Airlines levies cancellation charges and does not refund money if one misses a flight. Charges for cancelling tickets more than 48 hours ahead is Rs 20, between 24 and 48 hours it is 10 per cent of the fare and between one hour and 24 hours before the flight, 25 per cent. Consult the time table appearing every Monday in all Daily newspapers for dates and timings.

Travel out of India

There are no international airlines operating from Bangalore. But enquires may be made at Air India. *Tel 224143/239420.*

Reservations

Reservations can be made at large travel agencies and at the various airline offices. Indian Airlines now has computerised reservations (Vayudoot does not) but it would be wise to re-confirm tickets and double check flight timings before leaving for the airport.

Indian Airlines, Booking and Reservation Office, Cauvery Bhavan, District Office Road, *Tel 144/211914.* Airport enquiries, *Tel 566233 or 141.*

TRAIN

Travelling by train is very economical and one is able to see (especially on long distance journeys) the topography and culture of the various places. Five classes of passenger services are provided: airconditioned first class (almost as expensive as air travel), non-airconditioned first class, airconditioned second class (two-tier sleeper), ordinary second class (three-tier sleeper) and airconditioned chair car (with only the reclining seat accommodation). Food is usually served Indian style (though an Indian version of the western cuisine is available in the airconditioned first class) and orders can be placed with an attendant who comes round for this purpose. The quality of food and the time at which it is served varies considerably from sector to sector. It is a good idea to carry biscuits, cheese, fruits (one can also buy these on the platform) and snacks to supplement the food available on trains. Though aerated drinks, tea and coffee can be bought on the train and at most stations, carrying a good supply of boiled drinking water is a must. Bedding is provided in first class and second class a/c compartments but one has to ask the compartment superintendent for it preferably before the train leaves the station. It is often best to carry one's own pillows (inflatable ones are available all over India) and sheets, especially when travelling by ordinary second class. Not all ordinary second class coaches have cushioned seats and berths.

Indrail passes offering unlimited travel during the period of validity (varying from 7 to 90 days) are available to foreign nationals and non-resident Indians and are payable in foreign currency. These passes are available for different classes of travel. Child Indrail passes (for children between five and twelve yrs) are available at half rate. Children below five years of age are allowed to travel free of charge. Elderly persons above 65 years of age can avail of a 25 per cent discount in their fares. Reservation of tickets can be made upto six months in advance. (Consult *Tel 131/135*).

Cancellations

Cancellations of tickets more than two days before the date of the journey is at the rate of Rs 15 for a/c first class, Rs 10 non-a/c first class, second class a/c and a/c chair car, and Rs 5 for second class. Charges for cancelling tickets two days before the date of journey is half the fare subject to a minimum of Rs 60 for first class a/c Rs 30 for non a/c first class, second class a/c, and chair car, and Rs 15 for ordinary second class. (The rates are subject to change from time to time.)

City Railway Station : Reservation counters open from *0630 – 1315, 1345 – 2100.*
Enquiries and reservation second class : *Tel 132.*
Arrival and departure of trains at City Station : *Tel 133/134.*
Bangalore Cantonment Railway Station : *Tel 135.*
Bangalore East Railway Station : *Tel 571435.*
Yeshwantpur Railway Station : *Tel 361444.*
Other railway booking offices :

Shopping complex, IV block, Jayanagar, *0900–1200, 1400–1800.*
Sri Narasimha Raja Road, *0900–1200, 1400–1800.*
All cancellation of tickets should be carried out at the station where the ticket was booked.

ROAD

Bangalore is a focal point for a network of roads connecting it with major cities, towns and tiny villages all over India. The national highways and state highways are reasonably well maintained and pass through some scenic landscapes. This is true especially of Karnataka. By western standards driving in India is a hazardous task but it has its compensations by way of leisurely travel, exploring the country's many facets and meeting its people. Those who do not possess a vehicle have a choice of hiring cars and vans or travelling on KSTDC (Karnataka State Tourism Development Corporation) conducted bus tours, state owned inter-state long distance buses and buses run by private tour operators.

KSRTC

Cars and Vans

Chauffeur driven airconditioned and ordinary cars, vans and mini-buses (for larger groups) can be hired from approved travel agencies and taxi operators. The ITDC and KSTDC also offer cars on hire. The agencies offer a variety of rates and schemes so one could choose the most suitable one.

Excursions and Picnic Spots

Bangalore is surrounded by pleasant countryside, a patchwork of fertile fields and rocky, boulder-strewn landscapes which offer several attractive picnic and excursion spots. In most places food and accommodation are not provided. The KSRTC bus service is mentioned alongside each place.

Bannerghatta **C3 131**

The Bannerghatta National Park spread over 104 km and developed exclusively as a reserve for wildlife is situated about 21 km south of the city. Visitors can go round the park in vehicles to see the animals at close range. The park also has a serpentarium, a pets corner and a crocodile farm. Picnicking is allowed only in a specified area within the park.
Working hours : *0900–1200, 1400–1700.*
Vehicle charge : Rs 3 per adult, Rs 2 per child.
Bus service : Buses from main City Bus Station, from Kalasipalayam Bus Stand, and from Shivajinagar are available; *Tel 222722.*

Ramohalli **C3 131**

This is a picturesque picnic spot 24 km from Bangalore. It is the site of an ancient banyan tree spreading out to cover about four acres of land. It is supposed to be the biggest tree of its kind in Karnataka. The KSRTC is putting up a restaurant here.
B.T.S. buses from Kalasipalayam Bus Stand, *Tel 602177.*

Hessaraghatta **C2 131**

About 29 km from Bangalore is a large man-made lake covering about 1000 acres on which the Hessaraghatta Boat Club is located. (Sailing boats are available to members only). The Indo-Danish Dairy Project and the Government Horticultural and Dairy Farms are also located here. The lake and its attractive surroundings make Hessaraghatta a popular picnic spot. There is a Traveller's Bungalow, *Tel 2042.*
Reservation : Contact Chairman, Bangalore Water Supply and Sewerage Board (B.W.S.S.B), Kaveri Bhavan, *Tel 210563.*

Chamarajasagar Reservoir (Tippagondanahalli) **C2 131**

The Chamarajasagar Reservoir made by a dam across the River Arkavathi is about 35 km from Bangalore. The main purpose of the reservoir is to supply water to the city but it also makes an ideal picnic spot. Angling is permitted with prior permission. Accommodation is available at the Rest House.

Advance Reservation : Contact Chairman, Bangalore Water Supply and Sewerage Board, (B.W.S.S.B.), Kaveri Bhavan, Kempe Gowda Road, *Tel 210563.*

Channapattana **C3 131**

This town, 40 km along the Bangalore–Mysore road, is well known for its lacquerware and silk industries. The town is full of little shops selling lacquer bric-a-brac. Channapattana is also famous for its colourful wooden toys. The silk mill here produces saris and carpet yarn using silk waste.
Buses from the main Central Bus Station, *Tel 71261.*

Muthyala Maduvu (Pearl Valley)

This delightful picnic spot just 45 km from Bangalore is situated amidst hills near a shimmering waterfall which cascades some 90 m down the hillside. There is a small temple close by dedicated to Lord Shiva. Accommodation in the form of a Traveller's Bungalow is available at Anekal, 6 km away.
Advance Reservation : Contact Block Development Officer, Anekal.

Nandi Hills **D2 131**

Nandi Hills, a giant outcropping of rock, has been a favourite retreat since the time of the Ganga kings. Succeeding conquerors have left their mark on it. Two temples, the Yoga Nandishwara at the top of the hill and the Bhoga Nandishwara in the village of Nandi at the foot of the hill (both built in the eleventh century), are excellent examples of Chola art. The succeeding Hoysala and Vijayanagar kings renovated and enlarged them. Hyder Ali and Tipu Sultan elaborately fortified the hill. The ruins of the fortifications can still be seen today. The two rulers had a simple method of getting rid of enemies—they were pushed over a precipice aptly called Tipu's Drop. The equable climate on Nandi Hills made it a popular resort for British officers during the hot months; attractive bungalows dot the hillside. The hill offers a panoramic view of the surrounding countryside making it an excellent picnic spot. Viewing the sunrise and the sunset from the hill is an enjoyable experience.
Best season : March to mid-May.
Advance Reservation : Contact Director of Horticulture, Lal Bagh, *Tel 602231.*

Contact Manager, Hotel Mayura Pine Top, KSTDC, Nandi Hills.

Kanva Reservoir **C3 131**

The reservoir and its pleasant, peaceful surroundings make it a good picnic location. Accommodation is available at the Travaller's Bungalow.
Advance Reservation : Contact the Assistant Executive, No. 2 Subdivision, Channapattana, *Tel 362.*
Bus : KSRTC bus from main Bangalore Bus Station to Ramanagaram. Alight and change buses at Ramanagaram for Kanva Reservoir.

Mekedatu (Goat's Leap) **C3 131**

Ninetyeight kilometres from Bangalore the River Arkavathi makes a deep gorge in a rock. The gorge is narrow enough for a goat to jump from one bank to the other hence the name Goat's Leap. The Arkavathi joins the Cauvery river at Sangam about 5 km from here. There is a Traveller's Bungalow at Sangam.
Advance Reservations : Contact Assistant Engineer, No. 3 Subdivision, Kanakapura, *Tel 57.*

Kolar Gold Fields **D2 131**

Gold has been mined at the Kolar Gold Fields (98 km from Bangalore) for almost a century. K G F supplies all of India's gold. The Champion Reef Gold Mine with a depth of about 3030m is supposed to be the deepest working mine in the world. Visitors are allowed to go down into the mines with prior permission. Accommodation is available.
For permission and accommodation : Contact The Secretary, Bharat Gold Mines Ltd., Kolar Gold Fields.

Devaranyadurga **C2 131**

Devaranyadurga is a pleasant hill resort situated 80 km from Bangalore amidst wild and picturesque scenery and surrounded by an extensive forest. The town is named after Chikka Deva Raja Wodeyar who captured it in 1696 and whose fortifications can still be seen. Two temples dedicated to Ugra Narasimha and Bhoga Narasimha are also places of interest. Accommodation is available at the Forest lodge and Tourist Bungalows.

Advance Reservation: Traveller's Bungalow : Contact Assistant Engineer, No. 1 Subdivision, Public Works Department, Tumkur.
Tourist Rest House : Accommodation Manager, Department of Tourism, Devaranyadurga.

Kaiwara

According to legend Kaiwara (75 km from Bangalore) was earlier known as Ekachakrapura where the Pandavas in the epic *Mahabharata* stayed for a while during their exile. A cave located in a hill called Chikkabetta close to the town is believed to have been used by the demon Bakasura who was killed by Bhima. The Amaranarayana temple is worth seeing particularly for the carvings within the temple and the four black stone pillars that support the navaranga. Other temples in Kaiwara are the Bhimesvara, Sahadevesvara and Nakulesvara of which the Bhimesvara is the largest. The sculptures in the temple illustrate the story of Bhima's fight with Bakasura. The Travellers Bungalow at Chintamani provides accommodation.
Advance Reservation : Assistant Executive Engineer, Chintamani.

Shivaganga **C2 131**

Rising 4,559 feet above sea level is the hill of Shivaganga, a very popular pilgrim centre. It is 60 km from Bangalore. The hill is supposed to resemble different Hindu deities when viewed from different directions—a bull from the east, Ganesha the elephant headed god from the west, a serpent from the north and a linga from the south. The number of steps leading to the top of the hill is said to equal the number of 'yojanas' (leagues representing distance) from Shivaganga to Varanasi, so climbing it is believed to be equivalent to a trip to that holy city. For that reason Shivaganga is also called Dakshin Kashi.

There are several temples located on the hill but the Gangadhareshvara and Honna Devamma temples are the most interesting. Both are formed from large natural caverns with steep steps leading up to them. Close to the Honna Devamma temple is a deep cleft of rock through which a natural spring flows. According to a legend, on one occasion Parvati (consort of Shiva) felt thirsty and asked Shiva to release some water from the Ganga which he carried tied in the knot of hair on top of his head. When Shiva refused to do so she assumed the form of Honnadevi, an incarnation of Kali, and struck the rock with her sword. The water that gushed out of the rock is known as the 'Patala Ganga' or the Ganga of the nether regions.

Bus service : Buses from main City Bus Station, from Kalasipalayam Bus Stand, and from Shivajinagar are available; *Tel 222722.*

Places of Interest Outside Bangalore

Accessible from both Bangalore and Mysore are three famous tourist spots: the Jain pilgrimage centre of Shravanabelagola and the two exquisite Hoysala temples at Belur and Halebid. While most tourist buses from Bangalore and Mysore take one to these three places in just one tiring day it is also possible to see these places at leisure. The ideal place to begin and end the journey is Hassan, 185 km from Bangalore and 120 km from Mysore. From here Shravanabelagola is just 52 km away, Belur 40 km and Halebid 32 km, and all three places can be reached by bus. The Archeological Survey of India has appointed fast talking and remarkably informative guides at Belur and Halebid but there is no such service at Shravanabelagola. Although the guides are supposed to perform this service free of charge they usually ask for a small fee from each person.

The best way to get to Hampi (400 km north of Bangalore) is by rail to Hospet which is 13 km away from Hampi and connected to it by road. There are no tourist cottages or hotels here but there are a couple of guest houses and PWD inspection bungalows. Alternatively there are more places available for stay at the Tungabhadra Dam, 5 km from Hospet, including a KSTDC run hotel with rooms at moderate prices.

Hampi

Hampi Power House Guest Houses. Contact Superintendent Engineer, Hydroelectric Station, T B Board, T B Dam.
Public Works Department (PWD) Inspection Bungalow. Contact Assistant Engineer, PWD, No. 2 Subdivision, Hospet.

Tungabhadra Dam

Vaikunta Guest House, T B Dam. Contact Executive Engineer, HLC Division, T B Dam, via Hospet.
Inspection Bungalow. Contact Executive Engineer, HLC Division, T B Dam, via Hospet.
Hotel Mayura Vijayanagar, T B Dam.
Enquiries and Reservation : Tourist Officer, Tourist Bureau, KSTDC, 10/4 Kasturba Road, Bangalore, *Tel 212901.*

Hassan

Travellers Bungalow
Hassan Motel
Hotel Palika, *Tel 7145*
Hotel Sanman
Hotel Dwaraka
Sathyaprakash Hotel
Prashanth Tourist Home

Belur

KSTDC Tourist Cottages
Inspection Bungalow

Halebid

KSTDC Tourist Cottages
Travellers Bungalow

Shravanabelagola

Tourist Home. Enquiries and Reservation: KSTDC, St Mark's Road, Bangalore, *Tel 212901.*
Mysore Tourist Centre, J L B Road, Mysore, *Tel 30719.*

Shravanabelagola **B3 130**

Shravanabelagola meaning 'white pond of the ascetic'

nestles between two rocky hills 175 km west of Bangalore. The pond, long since dry, was substituted by a temple tank built by Chikka Deva Raja Wodeyar in the seventeenth century at the foot of the larger hill called Indiragiri or Doddabetta. Shravanabelagola dates back to the third century B.C. when Emperor Chandragupta Maurya gave up his empire and, accompanied by his guru Bhadrabahu Muni, settled here to lead the life of an ascetic. From that small beginning Jainism spread over the whole of south India and flourished under the Ganga rulers (fourth to tenth centuries A.D.) who ruled over the southern portion of what is now the state of Karnataka. Subsequent Hindu dynasties were tolerant of Jainism with the result that Shravanabelagola is now endowed with 37 bastis (temples) and an incredible 525 inscriptions. It has been the citadel of Jain culture for over 2000 years.

The town itself is small with a population of less than 5,000, but it contains some interesting monuments.

Bhandari Basti This is the largest temple in Shravanabelagola dedicated to the 24 Tirthankaras (Jain saints) and therefore also called 'Chaturvimsati Tirthankara Basti'. The 'garbha griha' (sanctum sanctorum) has three-foot high figures of the 24 Jain saints on a common ornamental pedestal. The temple is probably named after the 'bhandari' or treasurer of the Hoysala kings, who commissioned this temple.

Akkana Basti This temple is worth a look for its detailed sculpture and polished finish that is characteristic of the Hoysala school of architecture. The temple is dedicated to Parsvanatha (23rd Jain saint) whose idol is sheltered by a carved seven hooded serpent. The four navaranga (columned hall) pillars ornamented with beadwork are highly polished. The ceilings in the porch, the navaranga and the outer wall, decorated with pillars and miniature turrets, are of special interest.

Statue of Bahubali **B2 130**

The famous statue of Bahubali (or Gomateshvara as he is also called) is located at the top of Indiragiri. According to legend a bitter war of succession broke out between the two sons of Emperor Vrishabhadeva when he renounced his kingdom and took to a life of penance. Bahubali the elder son won the hard fought battle but at the moment of victory he realised, in a flash of revelation, the shallowness of the material world. He gave up his newly won kingdom to Bharatha his younger brother and took to the life of an ascetic beginning a thousand year penance. It is said that he stood motionless for so long that anthills formed at his feet and creepers grew around his body.

Soaring about 17.2m above the summit of the hill and carved out of a single, fine grained, light gray granite rock, Bahubali still continues his penance. The statue was commissioned by Chavundaraya, a general under King Rachamalla of the Ganga dynasty (fourth to tenth centuries A.D.) and carved by a famous court sculptor called Aristenemi. The simple sculpture, unmarked after all these centuries, was completed around 981 A.D. and is so perfectly proportioned that it remains in perspective, regardless of the angle from which it is viewed. The most interesting feature of the statue is the face, for despite its size (six feet and six inches from crown to the tip of the ear) it reflects a remarkable inner contentment and serenity.

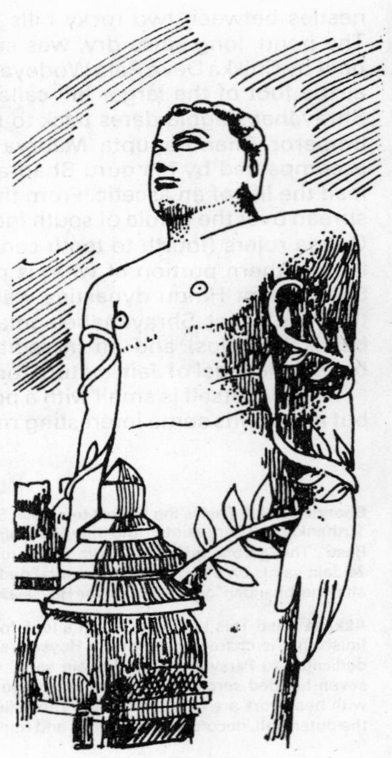

Gomateshvara

Strangely for a statue so perfectly sculptured, the forefinger of the left hand is shorter than it should be. There is a story that it was deliberately mutilated by the sage Ramanujacharya after he had converted the Hoysala king Vishnuvardhana to Hinduism, so as to make it unfit for worship. But the commonly held belief is that the statue was so perfect that a mutilation was necessary to ward off the evil eye!

Once in twelve years or so, 'at certain conjunctions of the heavenly bodies' the 'Mastakabhisheka' or the head anointing ceremony of Bahubali is performed, when the statue is bathed in milk, ghee, curds, vermillion, flowers, saffron, sandalwood, and finally silver and gold coins.

The other well known monuments on Indiragiri are :

Thyagada Brahmadeva Stambha (Pillar of sacrifices) Located three-fourths of the way up the hill, this 1.5m tall elegantly carved pillar is supported from above in such a way that a handkerchief can be drawn from under it. The Ganga general Chavundaraya is supposed to have sat here and donated alms to the poor.

Odegal Basti The largest basti on Indiragiri, it derives its name from the 'odegals' or stone props which strengthen its plain walls. The main shrine of this three-celled basti contains a polished black stone image of Vrishabhadeva, Bahubali's father and Adi Tirthankara, the first Jain saint.

The sister hill called Chandragiri, approximately 924m above sea level, is dotted with bastis and monuments mostly contained within a wall about 144m in length. Although built at different periods in history (the earliest one dates back to the eighth century A.D.) the temples are all built in the Dravidian style of architecture.

Chandragupta Basti is probably the smallest basti on the hill, measuring about 6.7m by 4.5m. This temple originally consisted of three cells in a row fronted by a narrow verandah. The centre cell contains a figure of Parsavanatha, the 23rd of the 24 Jain saints. An ornamental doorway was later put up in front of the verandah with perforated stone screens on the two sides. In the 45 interspaces on each screen are marvellously carved minute sculptures representing scenes from the lives of Chandragupta Maurya and his Jain guru Bhadrabahu. Traditionally supposed to have been built by Chandragupta Maurya and undoubtedly one of the oldest temples in Shravanabelagola (built sometime in the eighth or ninth century), the Chandragupta Basti probably got its name from the sculptures on the stone screens.

Bhadrabahu Cave Near the summit of the Chandragiri hill, is a cave named after Bhadrabahu Muni who is said to have attained nirvana here. The sage's footprints, carved on the stone floor of the cave, were supposedly worshipped by Chandragupta Maurya till his death after 12 years of penance.

Halebid

A2 130

Founded in the early eleventh century, Dwarasamudra (named after a lake besides which the city was founded) was the wealthy capital of the Hoysala kings till it was plundered twice by the marauding armies of Ala-ud-din Khilji in 1311 and Muhammad-bin-Tughlaq in 1327. The capital was then shifted to Belur and the place came to be known as 'hale bidu' or 'old capital'. Records kept by Muslim historians speak of the enormous wealth that was carried off by the armies and the splendour of the city before it was finally destroyed.

Around a small hill called Benne Gudda, portions of the old wall can still be seen as also the site of the palace to the east. South of the palace was the 'Ane Gundi' or elephant pit. The area on which the royal stables once stood is now under cultivation but is still entered in revenue accounts as laya (stables). The only portion of the city which escaped total destruction was the potter's lane. Legend has it that a potter gave shelter to a harried princess whose two rude sons were beheaded on the orders from an enraged royal concubine. In her anger the princess cursed the royal family and the city as well, predicting a speedy destruction of both, but sparing only the potter's lane.

Despite the curse and its subsequent repercussions in the form of the Delhi sultan's armies, the Hoysaleswara and Kedareswara temples, both dedicated to Shiva, survived the destruction.

The construction of the Hoysaleswara temple started a decade after the Chenna Kesava temple in Belur under the patronage of King Vishnuvardhana but after 80 years of labour it still remained incomplete. Situated in the middle of a beautifully maintained garden the larger Hoysaleswara temple is in a better state of preservation. Along with its two sister temples at Somnathpur and Belur this temple forms a 'golden triangle' of the best examples of one of the most prolific periods in south Indian temple architecture.

The twin-shrined temple is in the shape of a cross, with four doorways and beautifully carved lintels. In terms of workmanship the southern entrance is the loveliest. It was supposed to be used by the king when he visited the temple from his palace situated towards the southwest. A 3.3m high 'jagati' (parapet) running around the temple projects banded friezes of exquisite sculptures that is the hallmark of Hoysala architecture. Sturdy elephants form the bottom row followed by lions, amazingly intricate scroll work, and horsemen, supposed to symbolise the four qualities of stability, courage, beauty and speed necessary in a king. Above the horses the scroll work depicting scenes from the Puranas appears again. The topmost row consists of apsaras (celestial maidens) standing or seated under canopies decorated with beadwork. On the western wall of the temple the frieze takes on a different pattern. In place of the Puranic scenes is Hoysaleswara's 'piece de resistance'—the entire Hindu pantheon, complete with their many 'avatars' (incarnations).

Inside the temple, the twin shrines, exactly alike and crowded with intricate decorations, are separated by an intervening cell. Both navarangas (pillared halls) have columns supported by female bracket figures called 'madanakay', supposedly modelled after Ballala I's beautiful queen, Abhinava Ketala Devi.

The Jain bastis located some distance away from the Hoysaleswara, although considered plain compared to the intricate beauty of the Hindu temples are nevertheless remarkable in their own right. Of the original 720 bastis that were supposed to exist in Halebid at one time, only three survive now.

The temple to the west, called the Parsvanathesvara was built by Boppana, a general under the Hoysala kings, in 1133 A.D. and contains a 4.5m high image of Parsvanatha, the 23rd Jain saint. The navaranga boasts of a beautiful ceiling panel about 3.6m in diameter and highly polished lathe-turned black stone pillars decorated with beadwork. These pillars are peculiar to this temple although comparatively poorer imitations can be found in the navarangas of the Belur temples and the Akkana Basti at Shravanabelagola.

The small plain temple to the east of the Parsvanatheswara is dedicated to Adinatha, the first Jain saint. The original idol of Adinatha, a stout seated figure which had been mutilated, is now kept in the navaranga of the temple to its east.

Similar in plan to the first temple but without any embellishments whatsoever is a temple dedicated to Bantinatha. The idol is about 4.2m high and to facilitate the anointing of the image there are flights of steps on both sides of the idol.

Belur **A2 130**

Although over 800 years ago Belur was an important city under the Hoysalas, today the Chenna Kesava temple is the sole reminder of its glorious past. It was commissioned in 1117 by Vishnuvardhana, the Hoysala king, to commemorate his conversion from Jainism to Hinduism. Architecturally it has the same basic Hoysala pattern as its sister temples, but in the Chenna Kesava the builders reached the zenith of their exquisite craftsmanship.

Of the three entrances to the temple, the one to the east is perhaps the most beautiful. The doorjambs have the sculptured figures of Kama the God of Love and his consort Rati, to remind the devotee that he is still in the physical world of desires and emotions, all thoughts of which he must shed when he enters the Lord's presence. A jagati or parapet starts from the east entrance and runs along the walls of the temple, containing rows of elephants (of which no two are alike), stylised lion heads, intricate scrollwork containing tiny human figures in every possible posture, ornamental figures in projecting niches, separated by awesome 'yakshas' appropriately imbedded in the wall, and another row of ornamental figures. Along the upper edge of the caves runs a thick convoluted creeper. Of the 20 perforated stone screens which admit light into the temple, ten are sculptured. The two on either side of the eastern doorway represent scenes from the durbar of a Hoysala king, probably Ballala II; the rest depict scenes from the Puranas. Of particular interest in the Belur temple are 42 'madanika' or bracket figures, mostly of women, and so beautifully carved and finished that they seem almost alive. According to legend the model for these figures was Rani Shantala/Ketala Devi who were versatile in music and dance.

Madanika

The interior of the temple contains a similar profusion of sculpture and ornamentation. The large, elaborate ceiling panel in the centre of the navaranga is minutely carved and embellished with an eye for detail that is awe inspiring.

To a patient explorer, the carvings are all the more delightful for the everyday and therefore timeless situations they depict. For instance, the last figure on the left of the northern doorway represents a huntress flanked by two small figures, one of them carrying a bamboo pole to the ends of which are tied a deer and a crane, shot in the chase; the other figure is getting a thorn removed by a third person who is using a needle for the purpose. In the creeper-like canopy above is a perfectly sculptured ripe fruit with a fly on it and to complete the picture, a lizard nearby, ready to pounce.

The image that sits amidst this artistic profusion is that of Chenna Kesava meaning Handsome God. According to legend the idol was not carved along with the rest of the temple, but brought down from the Baba Budan hills. By an oversight, the idol of his consort was left behind. Kesava therefore has to visit her every once in a while, using a pair of large slippers kept for this purpose in the temple!

Hampi (Vijayanagar)

Vijayanagar, the capital city of a mighty Hindu empire of the same name, situated in 'one of the most spectacular natural settings' in the northern district of Bellary, was founded in 1336 by two local princes, Harihara I and Bukka.

At the height of its glory, the Vijayanagar empire stretched from the Arabian Sea to the Bay of Bengal and from the Deccan plateau to Kanyakumari in the south. In the 200 years before the empire was disempowered in 1565 by the combined forces of the Deccan Sultans of Bijapur, Bidar, Berar, Ahmednagar and Golconda, the Vijayanagar kings had succeeded in making their city a 'showpiece of imperial magnificence'. The kings were tolerant of other religions and were themselves neither completely Vaishanavite nor Shaivite with the result that the city was populated with people from a wide cross-section of linguistic, ethnic and religious backgrounds. Inevitably this had an impact on the city, particularly in the architectural styles.

Vijayanagar was at one time believed to have covered 33 sq km and can be divided into four zones : the natural rock outcropping on the south bank of the Tungabhadra on which there are numerous temples ; an 'urban core' within an elaborate defence fortification ; palaces, temples and other monuments used by the king, to the southwest of the urban core; and eventually the outlying portions of the capital.

Among the many temple complexes in Vijayanagar, the Virupaksha and Vittala are the most interesting. Virupaksha, also known as Pampapathy, an aspect of Shiva, is the consort of Pampa, a local goddess identified with the Tungabhadra river. The worship of Pampa and Virupaksha existed before the advent of the Vijayanagar kings; the older parts of the temple consisting of shrines grouped around a tank date back to the eleventh and twelfth centuries A.D., i.e. the late Chalukya and Hoysala periods. The temple was considerably enlarged and decorated by the Vijayanagar kings especially Krishna Deva Raya, who in 1512 commissioned the huge kalyana mantapa and the largest 'gopuram' (ornamental gateway) in the temple, which rises to over 50m. The kalyana mantapa is interspersed with richly adorned composite pillars typical of the Vijayanagar style, with animals and ornamental cornices. The unusual ceiling is painted, not carved, with scenes from the Shivapurana (the mythology of Shiva).

The Vittala temple complex commissioned by Krishna Deva Raya in 1513 contains six distinct structures. The temple in the centre, dedicated to Vishnu and built in the Dravidian style, consists of two mantapas; the pillars in the first hall are intricately carved out of single blocks of granite and each pillar comprises an entire sculptured group in itself. When tapped these amazing pillars emit musical tones.

East of this hall is the Garuda Mantapa, a miniature shrine in the shape of the chariots used during temple festivals. The other buildings of interest are :

The House of Victory (Mahanavami Dibba), built in 1516 A.D. by Krishna Deva Raya after his victorious expedition against the King of Orissa. The series of carvings around the platform seem to be unique in south India, and represent elephants, camels and horses along with wrestlers, boxers and dancing girls.

The Queen's Bath, built around a square tank, reflects a definite Islamic influence in its arches and projecting balconies.

The Lotus Mahal, built for an unknown purpose, is another perfect blend of Hindu and Islamic styles of architecture. This two storeyed pavilion is one of the most beautiful buildings in Hampi and provides an excellent example of the 'Vijayanagar courtly style' of architecture.

Principal Tourist Routes

With Bangalore as a base there is a wide choice of routes covering various parts of Karnataka. Although in each case the route outlined ends within the state boundaries, the journey can be terminated at Goa, Maharashtra, Andhra Pradesh, Tamil Nadu or Kerala. All routes begin from Bangalore since there are several major road and rail links to various parts of the state from here.

Route I offers an exhaustive and fascinating tour of Karnataka's temples built in different styles and dedicated to different gods. Some like Hampi and Badami are historical sites which ought not to be missed and are therefore mentioned in Routes II to V as well. Routes II to V cover hill stations, scenic spots, historical places, wildlife sanctuaries and beaches. These routes are merely suggested itineraries which may be used as a guideline, adding or leaving out places according to the time available. Places mentioned within parentheses are satellite places of interest which are a little away from the main route. The Govt. of India Tourist Office *(Tel 579517)* and the Dept. of Tourism, Govt. of Karnataka, *Tel 215883)* can be approached for help in working out individual itineraries.

ROUTE I : Temples in Karnataka

This tour begins and ends in Bangalore covering Karnataka in a wide anti-clockwise sweep.

Ghati Subramanya (52 km) **C2 131**

This famous temple dedicated to Subramanya with its impressive 'gopuram' (entrance tower) is 17 km northeast of Dodballapur. Choultries run by the temple authorities are available for staying overnight at this well known pilgrim centre.

Hampi (373 km)

This was once the glorious capital of a powerful Hindu empire that fell in the mid-sixteenth century. Hampi (or Vijayanagar as it was called) has several temples besides other buildings and monuments which are worth visiting. The temples built on the Hemakoota Hill are interesting examples of the medieval Deccan style of the ninth and tenth centuries, before the rise of the Vijayanagar kings. There are several magnificent temples built by the Vijayanagar kings—the Virupaksha temple complex which is the main shrine at Hampi and the Vittala temple complex famous for its mantap with musical columns.

Also of religious interest are *Sugriva's Cave* and the monolithic images of Ganesha and Narasimha.

The Lotus Mahal : The Lotus Mahal is one of the several beautiful buildings in Hampi. This two-storeyed structure on a stepped plane is a perfect example of the Vijayanagar country style and the fusion of Islamic and Hindu architectural styles.

The Lotus Mahal

Badami (516 km)

Badami and the two smaller towns of Pattadakal and Aihole to the northeast once formed the capital cities of the Chalukyas who ruled the Deccan between the fourth and eighth centuries A.D. The temples are built in the early Dravidian style. Several cave and rock temples reflect the Shaivite, Vaishnavite, Jain and Buddhist beliefs of the people in the Chalukyan times.

Aihole In and around Aihole are some 70 structures which almost cover the history of Hindu temple architecture from its genesis as exemplified by the Ladkan temple to the more complex stages as in the Kunthigudi and Durgigudi temples.

Pattadakal The capital of the Chalukyas between the seventh and eighth centuries Pattadakal was also the place where the Chalukya kings were coronated. Of the many temples here the Lokeshwari (or Virupaksha) temple and the Mallikarjuna temples are attractive structures.

Gadag (345 km)

Of the several temples in this town south of Badami, the most interesting is the intricately carved Trikuteshwara temple dedicated to Shiva. The name means 'Lord of the Three Peaks'. Within the temple compound is also the temple of Saraswati the main feature of which is a porch with elegant pillars.

Lakkundi, southeast of Gadag, has several interesting temples of which the Shiva temples of Kashi Vishwanath, Nandeswara and a beautifully carved ancient Ishwara temple built in the Hoysala style are worth visiting.

Harihar (270 km) **A1 130**

The Sri Harihareswara temple built in 1223 in the Hoysala style was later expanded in 1268 by Soma, the builder of the Somnathpur temple near Mysore. The idol is a rare one of Harihar—half Shiva and half Vishnu.

Sringeri (326 km) **A2 130**

A beautiful town in the Western Ghats, Sringeri is also an important centre of religious learning for orthodox Hindus and was founded by Adi Shankaracharya, an eighth century philosopher and saint. The Vidya Shankar Temple has beautifully carved pillars representing the different zodiac signs. There is also a temple dedicated to Sharada (Saraswati), the Goddess of Learning.

At short distances from Sringeri in south Kanara are several Jain pilgrim centres.

Karkal contains several temples and a statue of Lord Bahubali, 13m high, constucted around 1432.

Mudabidri There are 18 bastis or Jain temples in this town, the oldest is the Chandranatha temple which has a thousand richly carved pillars.

Venur A statue of Bahubali, 11m high, stands on the bank of the Gurupur river. There are also some Jain bastis and a Mahadeva temple which is now in ruins.

Dharmastala (286 km) **A2 130**

This is a famous pilgrim centre. Besides the numerous Jain bastis in this town, the Manjunatha temple is the most famous. A statue of Bahubali,14m high, was erected here in 1973.

Belur (222 km) **A2 130**

A beautiful Vishnu temple dedicated to Chenna Kesava is located here. It is the only one of the three famous Hoysala structures which still functions as a temple.

Halebid (216 km) **A2 130**

The first capital of the Hoysalas, what remains of it today is the exquisite Hoysaleswara temple dedicated to an aspect of Shiva. There are also three Jain bastis some distance away from the temple.

Shravanabelagola (160 km) **B3 130**

Although the main attraction here is the statue of Bahubali, 17m high, erected in 981 A.D. there are several other temples and monuments of interest. Once in 12–14 years the Mahamastakabhishekha ceremony is performed when the statue is bathed in yoghurt, ghee, sandalwood, gold coins, etc.

Melukote (156 km) **B3 130**

An important centre of Hindu learning, Melukote also has two Vishnu temples, the Sri Krishna and Sri Yoga Narasimhaswamy temples, which attract a large number of devotees. Each year in April the 'Vairamudi' festival takes place here.

Talkad (186 km) **C3 131**

Although many of the temples in this town are buried under sand there are several which can still be seen, amongst which the Kirtinarayana temple is the most interesting.

ROUTE II

The Kolar Gold Fields (96 km) **D2 131**

All of India's gold is supplied from the Kolar Gold Fields. The

Champion Reef Gold Mine, almost 3,300 m below the surface, is the deepest working mine in the world. Permission from the Secretary of the Mines is needed to visit the mine.

Lepakshi (104 km) **C2 131**

Although not strictly within the borders of Karnataka, Lepakshi is close to and easily accessible from Bangalore. The Veerabhadra temple with its giant Nandi (about 9 m long, India's largest) are definitely worth visiting. The place is also famous for its textiles.

Penukonda (60 km) **C1 131**

Less than two hours away from Lepakshi is an attractive hill station which contains fascinating ruins of the Vijayanagar empire.

Devarayanadurga (75 km) **C2 131**

This is a scenic hill station situated in wooded country. There are several temples dedicated to Narasimha, Vishnu's half-man, half-lion incarnation.

Shravanabelagola, Halebid, Belur (see places of interest outside Bangalore).

Kemmannugundi (257 km) **A2 130**

The serene hill station of Kemmannugundi lies in the heart of the Baba Budan range. The range got its name from a Muslim saint who is believed to have introduced coffee into India from Mecca.

Agumbe (357 km)

It is a tiny hill station in the Western Ghats. From here, the view of the sun setting in the Arabian Sea is breathtaking.

Udipi (381 km)

A town famous for its 'tiffin' (south Indian snacks), Udipi also has a thirteenth century temple dedicated to Sri Krishna.

Malpe 5 km from Udipi is Malpe, which has an attractive beach where swimming and fishing are permitted.

ROUTE III

Shivasamudram (122 km) **C3 131**

In Shivasamudram, an island town in the Cauvery river, are the twin waterfalls of Barachukki and Gaganachukki best seen in July and August. Situated here are two small but attractive temples dedicated to Shiva.

Somnathpur (137 km) **C3 131**

In the village of Somnathpur is an exquisite specimen of Hoysala temple architecture dedicated to Lord Kesava (Krishna). (See places of interest outside Mysore).

Somnathpur Temple

Mysore (140 km) **B3 130**

The seat of the erstwhile Wodeyar kings, this is a gracious city of palaces and gardens.

Shrirangapattana (14 km from Mysore) **B3 130**

This island was Tipu Sultan's capital, and his summer palace, a mosque and an ancient Vishnu temple dedicated to Lord Ranganatha still exist within the fort walls. Tipu's tomb is also situated here.

Ranganathittu Bird Sanctuary (16 km from Mysore)

The sanctuary is made up of many islets on the Cauvery river and is frequented by several species of water birds. **B3 130**

Brindavan Gardens (19 km from Mysore) **B3 130**

These gardens are laid out beside the Krishnarajasagar dam. Their terraces and fountains make it a delightful spot. (See places of interest outside Mysore).

Hunsur (175 km) **B3 130**

The site of the Tibetan refugee resettlement camp in Bylakuppa (25 kms) is called Rabagayling—'Good Progress Place'. There are two Tibetan monastries and two carpet factories which take individual orders. The traditional Tibetan fare of 'momos' and 'thuppa' (noodle soup) is served in this town.

Nagarhole Wildlife Sanctuary (240 km) **B3 130**

The Nagarhole wildlife sanctuary is situated on the Kerala border and consists of almost 200 species of birds and many species of animals, all in their natural habitat.

Madikeri (Mercara) (253 km) **A3 130**

The largest town in the Coorg region, Madikeri is surrounded by forests, coffee plantations and paddy fields. Above the town is a formidable fortress built by the Coorgi Rajas. Close to it is the Omkareswara temple with its unusual blend of Hindu and Islamic architecture.

Mangalore (357 km)

Mangalore has been a major sea port since Tipu Sultan's time and is still an important centre for the export of coffee and cashewnuts. Remnants of Tipu's fort called the Sultan's Battery, the old light house and the chapel of the St Aloysius College are worth seeing. The view from the top of the Kadri Hill is impressive.

Alternative routes Bangalore-Shivasamudram-Somnathpur-Mysore-Bandipur-Ooty (T.N.)

ROUTE IV: Up the Coast and Excursions Inland

From Mangalore Ullal, a pleasant seaside resort is a few kilometres south of Mangalore. There are several beach cottages here which provide accommodation.

Udipi, Malpe (See Route II)
Maravanthe (60 km), Less than two hours from Malpe is an excellent beach.

Kollur (80 km) About 80 km inland Kollur is famous for its Mookambika temple, which is said to be founded by Adi Shankaracharya.

Jog Falls Inland from Honavar (97 km from Marvanthe) are the Jog Falls formed by the Sharavati river, the highest in India with a drop of 253m. The four separate waterfalls are specially impressive during the rainy season.

Jog Falls

Magod Falls The smaller but equally beautiful Magod Falls created by the Gangavathi river plunging 183 m down a deep gorge is to the north of Jog Falls and is approached through Sirsi (80 km from Honavar). There is a KSTDC Tourist Home here.

Dandeli Wildlife Sanctuary Sandwiched between two rivers 90 km north of the Magod Falls is the Dandeli Wildlife Sanctuary. In this thick forest rich in teak and bamboo, wild animals can be seen from inside vehicles. Fishing is allowed in the Kali river.

Karwar (378 km)

Karwar, which is on the west coast, was supposed to have been visited by Vasco da Gama in the fifteenth century. Besides its excellent beaches there is also the fort on Sadashivgad, and the lighthouse both of which are worth a visit.

Ankola About 37 km south of Karwar is Ankola, a little village where the fifteenth century Sri Venkataramana Temple and the ruins of a fort built around the same time can be seen. A few kilometres south of Ankola is an important pilgrimage spot, the Mahabaleshwara temple in the village of Gokarna.

The National Highway (N.H.) 17 from Karwar leads to Panaji in Goa.

ROUTE V

Chitradurga (200 km) **B1 130**

Chitradurga on the road to Hampi has a famous seventeenth century fort built by Nayak Pallegars (chieftains) of that region.

Hampi (350 km)

The capital of the Vijayanagar kings from the fourteenth to the sixteenth centuries, Hampi has a wealth of architecture to offer the visitor. Enormous temples built in the Dravidian style and airy buildings reflecting a fusion of Hindu and Islamic styles of architecture are of special interest.

Tungabhadra Dam (350 km) The Tungabhadra Dam close to Hampi offers a quiet spot for relaxation.

Raichur (476 km)

This was the capital of Bijapur for a short while before it came under the domain of the Vijayanagar empire. It has a fort with an enormous gate; the citadel inside offers a fine view from its top.

Gulbarga (584 km)

Gulbarga was the capital of the Muslim Bahamani kingdom between 1347 and 1428. Although the old fort is largely in ruins there are several interesting buildings inside and amongst them the Jami Masjid, supposedly built by a Moorish architect, is modelled on the mosque in Cordova in Spain. There are also several tombs of Bahamani kings and a temple.

Bidar (669 km)

The capital of the Bahamani kingdom from 1428 onwards, Bidar has an old fifteenth century fort within which there are several palaces. The tombs of the Bahamani kings are also worth seeing.

The National Highway 9, south of Bidar, leads to Hyderabad in Andhra Pradesh and to Solapur in Maharashtra in the west.

From Hampi

Bijapur (579 km)

Bijapur offers a complete contrast to Hampi, being a city with a predominantly Muslim history . Bijapur contains several mosques, palaces, fortifications and mausoleums, the most famous mausoleum being the Gol Gumbaz. Other places of special interest in Bijapur are the Ibrahim Roza, the Jami-e-Masjid, Asar Mahal, and an enormous cannon called

Gol Gumbaz

the Malik-e-Maidan. The Karnataka State Road Transport Corporation runs a bus service between *0800–2000* every *Sat–Sun* which takes visitors to the following places : Pattadakal, Shivayoga Mandir, Banashankari and Badami.

Belgaum (502 km)

In Belgaum, near the border with Goa, is a mosque built in 1519 and two Jain temples which have some fine carvings. To the northeast of Belgaum are the Gokak Falls where the Ghataprabha river drops down 52 m. The National Highway 4 which runs through Belgaum leads to Pune.

ROUTE VI

This covers sanctuaries and scenic spots within the state.

Ranganathittu Waterbird Sanctuary (19 km from Mysore)

B3 130

The sanctuary is made up of many islets through which the Cauvery flows. Of the several species on view here herons, ibis, jacanas, egrets and water fowl are the most conspicuous. Boats are available for rowing around the islets, which allows a close and memorable view of the birds.

Bandipur Wildlife Sanctuary

Situated at the foothills of the Nilgiris (Blue Hills) this thickly wooded, lush sanctuary covers an area of 865 sq km south of the Kabini river. The sanctuary has a large number of spotted deer, wild boar, sambar, gaur and cheetah. Bandipur comes under the jurisdiction of the Project Tiger. So these magnificent endangered animals can occasionally be spotted here. A variety of reptiles, birds and butterflies can also be found here. Tours on elephants and in forest jeeps and vans are available.
Season : *Jan–Jun, Sep–Oct.*

Mudumalai Sanctuary

Across the border in Tamil Nadu is the Mudumalai Sanctuary which is an extension of the Bandipur forest separated by the Periyar river. Here there are elephants, Indian bison, sambar, mouse deer, giant malabar squirrels, wild boar, gaur, chital and several varieties of reptiles.
Season : *Jan–Jun, Sep–Oct.*

Nagarhole Wildlife Sanctuary (240 km from Bangalore, 67 km from Mysore) **B3 130**

Situated to the north of the Kabini river on the border with Kerala, Nagarhole abounds in wildlife including tigers, leopards, elephants and deer. There are excellent hunting lodges for accommodation and elephant and jeep rides into the forest. One can also float down the Kabini in basket-like boats lined with buffalo hide. About 200 species of birds also find sanctuary here.

Kakanakote (73 km from Mysore)

Kakanakote is a luxuriant forest famous for the size and strength of the elephants found here. The Kabini river flows through the forest and offers a unique chance to watch wildlife while gliding silently over the water in a coracle.
Season : *Sep–Jun.*

Mysore Introduction

Set amidst rolling green countryside Mysore ('Mahisur' or Buffalo town) was named after the buffalo-headed demon Mahishasur who was defeated by Chamundi (an aspect of Parvati, consort of Shiva). Pleased with her victory and attracted by the beauty of the countryside Chamundi made the hump-backed hill her abode. The Chamuṇdi Hill, the abode of Chamundeswari, the deity of the Mysore kings, is an attractive landmark in Mysore.

Associated with Mysore since the beginning of the sixteenth century the royal Wodeyar family is as synonymous with the city as Kempe Gowda is with Bangalore. Following several undistinguished Wodeyars who accepted the suzerainty of the Vijayanagar kings through their viceroys in Shrirangapattana, Raja Wodeyar in 1610 captured Shrirangapattana and made it his capital. He built Mysore into a large and powerful kingdom. His weak and ineffectual successors, however, allowed power to slip into the hands of Hyder Ali and his son Tipu Sultan whose brief but tumultuous reign resulted in power being transferred to the victorious British in 1799. Restored to the throne by the British, Krishnaraja Wodeyar III's long reign was devoid of power. It was only during his successor Chamarajendra Wodeyar's rule that the administration of the state was handed back to the sovereign, aided of course by the British Resident in Mysore. To make up for lost time the period, beginning from the ascension of Chamarajendra Wodeyar to the throne (1881) till Independence

(1947), saw the growth of stately buildings and liberal policies, making Mysore one of the most progressive and attractive cities at that time.

Although Chamarajendra Wodeyar was the nominal head of government and Mysore the centre of administration, the real administrative power had shifted to Bangalore during Krishnarajendra Wodeyar's reign in the nineteenth century. Consequently Mysore was relegated to second place after Bangalore. The latter was declared the capital of the state of Mysore (later Karnataka) soon after Independence.

In contrast to busy, bustling modern Bangalore, Mysore's gentle, easy-going nature and old world charm is especially attractive. Regal turn-of-the-century buildings complement slow moving horse-drawn carriages and nonchalant cows on the roads. Individual bungalows have not as yet given way to highrise buildings and multi-storeyed flats.

Mysore is one of the few places where you can shop straight off the shop floor—literally! The government silk weaving factory and sandalwood oil factory are renowned for the famous Mysore silk saris, the equally famous aromatic 'agarbathis' (incense sticks) and 'attars' (extracts). One can buy all of these from the showrooms attached to the factories. Beautifully carved articles in sandalwood and rosewood, often with ivory inlay, ranging from little boxes to entire dining sets are also available in Mysore.

Industry in Mysore until some years ago consisted mainly of the production of handicrafts, silks and fragrances. Recently several industries engaged in the production of foods and beverages, tyres, electrical grade insulation boards, etc. have been started on the outskirts of the city.

Within reach of the city are one bird and three wildlife sanctuaries, towns of historical and architectural interest, several delightful picnic spots, and hill resorts in the Nilgiris (Blue Mountains) the drive to which is an enchanting experience in itself.

The Dussehra celebrations in September/October transform the city into a fairyland. The colourful processions, the music and dance, the display of fireworks and the beautifully lighted palace recreate the splendour of a bygone era.

Mysore can also lay claim to several other distinctions. The finishing touch of elegance for a gentleman in Karnataka is the Mysore turban while to a lady no sari collection is complete without one in Mysore silk. Ideally a meal which includes Mysore 'rasam' ought to be finished with delicious, crumbly Mysore 'pak'. And what could look better on a wall than a picture of the Mysore school of painting? Exploring this city with its fascinating history and discovering its charm is an unforgettable experience.

Gazetteer

Mysore is a small city by Indian standards and can be divided into two zones, north and south, by the Vinoba Road and Nazarbad Main Road.

The places of interest have been arranged in a logical order. Distances being relatively small, it is quite possible to combine both zones if one is energetic and enthusiastic enough!

As in Bangalore, autorickshaws are the best mode of transport although buses also operate within the city.

A system of three stars will serve as a guide for those who would like to see only the main sights.

Distances are measured from the main palace which is in the centre of the city. All roads lead to the palace.

North Zone (north of Vinoba Road, Nazarbad Main Road)

* **Government House** (3 km) **B1 186**

This lovely building served as the Mysore Residency in the nineteenth century. Unfortunately it is now a government guest house and has been stripped of much of its original furniture and fittings. It was built in 1805 by Major Wilks, the historian–administrator and Resident of Mysore, and is of the Doric order of architecture. A few years later his successor John Malcolm added a hall as a gift to his bride. This is one of the largest rooms without pillars in southern India, designed by the engineer, De Havilland. The semi-circular verandah leading from the banquet hall looks out over terraced gardens in the south.

Bus : 12, 25, 28, 51, 53, 73, 125.

**St Philomena's Church (now known as St Joseph's Cathedral) (4 km) B1 186

In a city whose chief charm lies in its buildings which are often eclectic in their mixture of styles the St Philomena's Church stands out sharply in contrast. The largest church in south India, it was built as a miniature reproduction of the Cologne Cathedral by Rev. Rene Feuga, Bishop of Mysore in the early 1930s. The whitewashed walls and high, vaulted Gothic ceiling impart a pearly white ambience to the inside of the church. Colourful stained glass representations, depicting the birth of Jesus, the Last Supper, the Crucifixion, the Resurrection and the Ascension of Christ allow light to stream into the church.

The catacomb under the altar features a reclining statue of

St. Philomena's Church

St Philomena and is regularly visited by devotees from all regions. A large organ situated in a gallery above the nave is another item of interest. The church, about 50m in length, has twin spires about 50m in height. The three bells which ring for Sunday service are located in the spires.

Bus : 125, 12, 73, 51, 53, 25, 28.

* St Bartholomew's Church (2 km) **B2 186**

Built along simple classical lines, the St Bartholomew's Church can be mistaken for a gracious private house but for the cross mounted on the roof. The church was built in 1832 on land donated by Krishnaraja Wodeyar III to serve the civil and military officers attached to the Residency. Despite its size the church twice played host to the visiting British Royalty - Prince Albert Victor in 1889, and the future King George V and his consort in 1906.

At the west end of the church over the altar is a large stained glass window depicting St Bartholomew. This was donated by Krishnaraja Wodeyar IV to mark the centenary of the church in 1930. The marble altar and rich teakwood panelling were also installed around this time.

Bus : 8, 23, 62, 31, 32, 33 and all buses to the mofussil bus stand.

Chamarajendra Statue

** Chamarajendra Statue (1/4 km) **B2 186**

In front of the northern gate of the palace at the junction of Ashoka Road and Albert Victor Road is the white marble statue of Chamarajendra Wodeyar erected in the 1920s. It was sculpted by Robert W Colton who spent a preliminary three months in Mysore researching it. It is worth a perilous dash across the busy roads that surround it to admire its beauty. The Indo-Saracenic style canopy stands on a granite base but the pedestal, four columns, elaborately carved brackets, sunshade and parapet are complementary in marble capped by a gleaming, gilded, ribbed, onion dome.

All buses to city bus stand.

* Krishnaraja Statue (1/4 km) **A2 186**

The Krishnaraja statue stands at the intersection of the Sayyaji Rao, Albert and Devraj Urs Roads, the vortex of a busy,crowded commercial area. Unveiled in 1952 the marble statue of this very popular maharaja is housed beneath a brick and masonry onion-ribbed dome on cusped arches supported by ornamental granite columns.

All buses to city bus stand.

* Clock Tower (1/4 km) **B2 186**

This was erected in 1927 by the servants and officers of the palace to commemorate 25 years of the reign of Krishnaraja Wodeyar IV. This four storeyed Indo-Saracenic style structure carries a touching message—'His Highness may be blessed with a long life and his reign rendered radiantly happy, memorable and prosperous.' The clock on the third floor of the tower was once part of the Dufferin Clock Tower built in 1886 to commemorate the visit of the Viceroy Lord Dufferin. The tower was demolished some years later but the clock was transplanted to this more permanent edifice.

Bus : 7, 22, 25, 28.

D1 185

** Central Food Technology Research Institute (3 km)

The 150 acre campus of the CFTRI was once the residence of the Princess Cheluvambamani Avaru, sister of Krishnaraja Wodeyar IV. The baroque European Renaissance style palace, profusely ornamented with pilaster work and lovely mosaic flooring, houses one of the country's most active centres for the research and development of post-harvest science and technologies. It offers a two-year course as well as shorter refresher courses in food technology and has been an associate institution of the United Nations University since 1976. The palace, situated at the summit of a low swell of land, provides a magnificent view of the Chamundi Hill.

The CFTRI guided tour offers a glimpse into their activities in the areas of food processing, protein-rich food supplements, concentrates, baby foods, etc; *open 1100–1300* and *1500–1800; contact PRO, Tel 22660.*

Bus : 4, 5, 18, 20, 21, 39, 70, 150, 30, 10.

** Railway Museum (3 km) **D1 185**

Rail buffs and tourists alike will find a visit to the railway museum (opposite the CFTRI on Krishnaraja Sagar Road) a rewarding experience. The museum contains exhibits from the Mysore State Railways which operated between 1881 and 1951. Among the exhibits are steam engines, signals and a Maharani's coach, complete with toilet, built in 1888; *open 1000–1300, 1500–2000; closed on Mon.*

Bus : 4, 5, 10, 29, 30, 18, 20, 21, 39, 70, 150

South Zone (south of Vinoba Road, Nazarbad Main Road)

* Zoo (2 km) **C3 187**

The Mysore Zoo was started by Chamarajendra Wodeyar in 1892 on about 10 acres of his property. Since then the zoo has considerably expanded. It now spreads over 250 acres and is the fourth largest zoo in India. The zoo has done away with iron bars of old-style zoos and efforts have been made to create a natural habitat for various animals and birds. An artificial lake called the Karanji Tank attracts a large number of birds—so far twenty-six different species have been spotted. The zoo has also been able to breed an impressive number of rare and endangered animals in captivity; *open 0830–1730; Sun 0900–1930; closed on Fri.*

Bus : 70, 71, 74, 101, 140, 9, 24, 75.

*** Mysore Palace **A2 186**

In 1897 a conflagaration destroyed the wooden palace which

had been rebuilt in 1800 after Tipu Sultan razed the original one to the ground. The Maharani Vanivilasa Sannidhana, wife of Chamarajendra Wodeyar and regent to Krishnaraja Wodeyar IV, decided to build a new palace in its place. It was designed by Mr Henry Irwin, architect of the Viceregal Lodge in Simla and at that time Consulting Architect with the Government of Madras.

This incredible building, measuring about 76m in length and about 44m from the ground to the golden flag on the main dome, is built in gray granite. Although the overall appearance and outline is Indo-Saracenic the wealth and delicacy of details within the palace is distinctly Hoysala in character.

Main Gate, Mysore Palace

The Palace is built around a 'thotti' (courtyard) which is open to the sky, south of which is the 'Kalyana Mantapa' or the marriage hall. Along the walls, painted on canvas in 26 panels, are Dussehra murals which capture the faces and costumes of the people who took part in the procession.

The designs on the octagonal stained glass dome supported by groups of three cast iron pillars were designed by Mysore craftsmen and made by the Walter McFarlene Saracen Foundry in Glasgow. On the first floor the long (about 47m) collonaded Durbar Hall for public audiences leads to the incredibly opulent Amba Vilas reserved for private audiences —with its carved teakwood ceiling, semi-precious inlay work in the Agra style on the white marble floor, doors of solid silver salvaged from the old palace, teakwood doors inlaid with ivory, and many chandeliers.

During Dussehra the Golden Throne of the Wodeyar kings is put on display in the Amba Vilas. According to legend the throne originally of figwood overlaid with ivory was discovered by Harihara and Bukka, founders of the Vijayanagar empire when the sage Vidyaranya pointed out the spot where it was buried. Since then it has been handed down from one dynasty to another and ultimately came into the possession of a Wodeyar ruler. It was used for the coronation of Krishnaraja Wodeyar III. Since then the throne has been covered with gold and silver plating. A mythical bird called the 'hamsa' (swan) surmounts the throne—legend has it that the person on whom its shadow falls will wear a crown.

There is a free guided tour of the palace every hour from 10 o' clock onwards: *open 1000–1600.*

All buses to city bus stand.

Surrounding the palace and within the fort walls are five temples :

**** The Varahaswami Temple** named after an incarnation of Vishnu is near the south gate. The image donated to a newly built temple in Shrirangapattana by Chikka Deva Raja Wodeyar in the late seventeenth century, was shifted to Mysore when the temple was demolished by Tipu Sultan. Purnaiya, Dewan to Krishnaraja Wodeyar III, built this temple with materials taken from a Hoysala structure.

*** The Lakshmiramana Temple** to the west is the oldest amongst the five having been in existence even before 1499. Legend has it that Raja Wodeyar who ruled in the early seventeenth century was served poison in the form of holy water by a priest who was paid to do so. The king swallowed it but came to no harm because of his firm faith in Vishnu, the chief deity of this temple.

Trinesvara Temple This Shiva temple to the south is built in the Dravidian style. It was renovated by Dodda Deva Raja Wodeyar who also commissioned the Nandi statue on Chamundi Hill.

**** The Prasanna Krishnaswami Temple** was built by Krishna Raja Wodeyar III in 1829. This Vishnu temple has a small cell in the 'prakara' (enclosure) of the temple enshrining a figure of sage Atri from whom the Wodeyars are supposed to have descended.

*** The Prasanna Venkataramanaswami Temple** was built in 1836 by a king's officer named Subbarayadasa. This Vishnu temple contains paintings of 12 Wodeyar kings as well as inscriptions giving their names and the period of their reign.

** Jagan Mohan Palace ($^1/_2$ km) **A2 186**

The facade of this colourful baroque building with domes, cuppolas and finials is a highly imaginative creation. This three-storeyed palace, now part auditorium and part museum, was built over a period of years since 1861. Marriages, a coronation and even birthday and Dussehra durbars were held here till the new palace was completed in 1910. The museum at the back contains bric-a-brac from the various palaces but the armoury and musical instruments sections are interesting. There is a beautiful collection of ivory articles. The paintings by Ravi Varma (on the 3rd floor) and Nicholas Roerich are of special interest; *open 1000–1300 and 1500–1700; closed on Mon.*

Bus : 54, 10, 27, 61

** Manasa Gangotri (Mysore University) (4 km) **B2 184**

The sprawling campus of the Mysore University used to be called Gordon Park after Sir James Gordon, tutor and guardian to Chamarajendra Wodeyar and subsequently the British Resident of Mysore in 1881. The Maharaja's College in Mysore and the Central College in Bangalore formed the nucleus of the Mysore University which was begun in 1916. At present the University comprises 123 colleges including evening colleges and the Institute of Correspondence Courses and Continuing Education. The University offices are housed in the imposing Crawford Hall with a plasterwork statue of Saraswati, Goddess of Learning, embossed on the pediment. Many of the buildings within the University grounds are architecturally interesting. A drive around the campus is a pleasant experience.

Bus : 29, 30, 35, 36, 71

Athara Kutchery : Within the Manasa Gangotri campus is the lovely white edifice of the 'Athaara Katcheri' (district offices). It was built in 1887, the jubilee year of Queen Victoria, and served as the office of the British Chief Commissioner of Mysore.

This European style two-storeyed building is surmounted by a central octagonal dome and finial adding to the height and grace of the building. The State of Mysore was the first in the country to have a representative government; from 1895 till 1923 the Representative Assembly held its annual meetings in one of the two halls in this building.

Oriental Research Institute : Within the campus is the Oriental Research Institute housed in the Victoria Jubilee Hall. This was built in the European style between 1887 and 1891 to commemorate the 50 years of Queen Victoria's reign. The juxtapositioning of Ionic and Corinthian pilasters with plaster bas reliefs depicting scenes from Hindu mythology are interesting.

The institute founded in 1891 was set up to preserve ancient manuscripts and to bring out publications of rare and valuable works. The institute today has a carefully preserved collection of 16,000 manuscripts and over 20,000 printed volumes. Besides manuscripts the institute also has stone inscriptions (twelve of which are set into the walls of the building) from the Chola, Hoysala and Vijayanagar periods including one on a decorated stone bed said to have once belonged to Kempe Gowda I, the founder of Bangalore. **D2 185**

** Government Silk Factory (5 km) **B1 188**

The Government Silk Factory on Madhwacharya Road is one

of four such factories in Karnataka which produce silk fabrics. The power looms in the factory spin an incredible 350 saris a day. Unfortunately the factory does not offer a guided tour.

As a symbol of the purity of their silk the Karnataka Silk Industries Corporation (KSIC) logo features a mythical bird called the 'hamsapakshi' (swan) which had the ability to drink only the milk from a bowl in which diluted milk was offered. The attached showroom has a well stocked collection of saris made in the factory; *open 0800–1200; 1500–1700.*

Bus : 1, 2, 6

** Government Sandalwood Factory (6 km) **B2 188**

A short walk futher along Madhwacharya Road and enveloped in fragrance, is the Government factory where sandalwood oil is extracted for use in soaps and perfumes. One can watch incense sticks, another famous product of Mysore, being made here mostly by women and children. Thin sticks, a little over six inches in length, are covered at one end with a putty made of sandalwood paste, dipped into little piles of incense and laid out to dry. The sales counter at the factory sells excellent sandalwood oil and some good incense sticks; *open 0900–1100; 1400–1600.*

Bus : 1, 2, 6

** Chamundeshwari Temple (13 km by road, 4 km by foot) **A3 190**

An important spot in Mysore the Chamundeshwari temple on top of Chamundi hill takes its name from the Goddess Chamundi, an aspect of the consort of Shiva, who defeated the demon Mahishasura and settled here.

Built in the twelfth century the Chamundeshwari temple, a fine quadrangular structure, is representative of the Dravidian school of architecture. In 1827 Krishnaraja Wodeyar III renovated the temple considerably and furnished it with a 'vimana' or tower over the sanctum sanctorum.

Chamundeshwari was also the ruling deity of the Mysore kings. The legendary ten day battle and her ultimate triumph over Mahishasura is celebrated every year in Mysore during Dussehra.

During this ten day festival music and dance programmes, exhibitions and sporting events are enthusiastically attended by large crowds. The Dussehra procession on the tenth day (Vijayadasami), in which the erstwhile Mysore maharajahs

Chamundeshwari

used to take part seated on a palace elephant in a golden howdah, is a much anticipated event.

Bus : 101

*** Mahabaleshwara Temple** South of the Chamundeshwari temple is the tiny Shiva temple of Mahabaleshwara. Although the more popular Chamundeshwari temple has relegated it to religious obscurity, the Mahabaleshwara is interesting from the historical point of view. A large number of inscriptions have been found in the temple and on the brass plated doorways. The oldest of these dates back to about 950 A.D., during the reign of the Gangas.

**** Nandi Statue** Three-quarters of the way up the Chamundi Hill is the monolithic statue of the Nandi bull which according to legend was completed in one night. The work is attributed to Dodda Deva Raja, an extremely devout Wodeyar king who ascended the throne in 1659. A flight of one thousand steps leading to the top of the hill was also commissioned by him.

Bus : 101 **A2 190**

Nandi

*** Rajendra Vilas** (13 km) **A2 190**

Built within the first decade of this century by Krishna Raja Wodeyar IV the Indo-Saracenic style Rajendra Vilas (now a hotel) is yet another royal residence in this city of palaces. Perched atop the Chamundi Hill it looks out over the Mysore countryside for miles around. Large mirrors, an arrangement of spears and shields and a pair of enormous tusks decorate the foyer.

Bus : 101

**** Lalith Mahal** (5 km) **B3 192**

Situated on rising ground to the east, beyond the crowded clutter of the city, the Lalith Mahal Palace (now an ITDC hotel) is one of the landmarks of Mysore. It is approached by a long curving road that gives the visitor ample time to admire its white, graceful lines.

The palace was designed by E W Fritchley and built by Krishna Raja Wodeyar IV in 1921 as a guest house for his European guests. The central dome is said to have been modelled on the lines of St Paul's Cathedral in London. The palace abounds in a number of minor ornamentations found in various palaces in Britain. Despite being converted into a hotel in 1974 the Lalith Mahal still projects a faintly royal ambience mainly because of the full length portraits of the Wodeyar kings, the gracious sweep of the Italian marble staircase, the Belgian cut glass lamps, heavy ornate furniture, mosaic tiles and a couple of exquisite Persian carpets. Both the Banquet Hall, a popular venue for conferences and the Ball Room, now a restaurant, have polished wooden flooring and three stained glass domes in the ceiling. The balcony upstairs affords a gorgeous view of Chamundi Hill to the left and the city of Mysore spread out below.

Bus : 9, 24, 75, 74, 70, 71, 140 to Teresian College and a one km walk from there.

Tourist Information Bureaus

KARNATAKA STATE TOURISM DEVELOPMENT CORPORATION (KSTDC)

Transport Wing,
Hotel Maurya Hoysala, Jhansi Lakshmibai Road,
Mysore - 570 005 *Tel 23652.*

Deputy Director of Tourism
Regional Tourist Office, Old Exhibition Building,
Mysore - 570 021 *Tel 220096.*

Transport

As in Bangalore the best mode of transport in Mysore is the autorickshaw which is available in plenty. The bus service is adequate and fairly punctual but most taxis in Mysore carry only cargo.

Bus

The city bus service operates from the City Bus Stand on Albert Victor Road in the heart of the city. The buses cover about 150 routes from *0600–2315* every day. The major areas in the city are well connected by a number of buses plying along different routes. Being a compact city Mysore can be traversed by bus from end to end in about 20 minutes even allowing for frequent stops to pick up passengers! Peak office hours *(0900–1015* and *1645–1830)* should be avoided. There are no night bus services or ladies specials but a limited stop service operates on some routes. An excellent bus guide and good bus timetables are available at the City Bus Stand (enquiries *Tel 20853*).

A suburban bus service also operates from the CBS (enquiries *Tel 23602/25819*), and provides cheap transport to places like Shrirangapattana, Krishnaraja Sagar and Chamundi Hill.

Mofussil buses run by the Karnataka State Road Transport Corporation (KSTDC) on Church Road operate within and outside the state of Karnataka.

Autorickshaw

Autos are a convenient way of getting around Mysore and are easily available. As in Bangalore there are no major language barriers as most auto drivers understand Hindi and simple English.

During night shifts *(2200–0000)* the autos charge one and a half times the normal meter reading. While getting in ensure that the meter is set at the minimum fare, i.e. Rs. 4.00. It is advisable that one mentions a prominent landmark close to one's destination (e.g., a cinema, garden or main street) if the driver seems uncertain.

Waiting charge usually is: first five minutes free and 50 paise for every 15 minutes, or a fraction thereof. One should be firm if the driver demands excess fare for reasons except those given above. The police in Mysore are helpful and friendly so one shouldn't hesitate to request police assistance; usually just threatening to call the police does the trick!

One can also hire an auto for the whole day. Mysore being a small city a fixed sum can be negotiated which usually works out to about Rs 100. Auto stands are located all over the city at convenient spots.

Car-hire

Chauffeur driven ordinary and airconditioned cars though expensive are a reasonable proposition if four or five people are sharing costs. Larger parties can travel in vans and mini-buses. Several hotels have a travel agency located within or close to the premises which will make the necessary arrangements. The KSTDC and other approved tourist car and van operators also have vehicles for hire.

Conducted Tours

The KSTDC and several other agencies listed in the Directory offer guided sightseeing tours of Mysore and other tourist spots. One can also sightsee at a leisurely pace in hired cars with guides who speak English, Hindi, and certain foreign languages, arranged through the Government of India Tourist Office; Karnataka State Tourism Department, Old Exhibition Building, Irwin Road, *Tel 22096*; or approved travel agents. Rates for the guides are fixed by the tourist offices.

Not all guided tours include extras such as entry fee to monuments, museums and meals in their fare charge. It is advisable to check up on what one is entitled to when buying the ticket.

KSTDC Tours

Mysore: Daily *0745–2030*. Chamarajendra Art Gallery in Jagan Mohan Palace, Zoo, Chamundi Hill, Somnathpura, Main Palace, St Philomena's Church, Shrirangapattana, Brindavan Gardens.

Ooty (via Bandipur) *0700–2130*. In Ooty : Botanical Gardens, Ooty Lake, shopping.

Temple Tour–Belur, Halebid, Shravanabelagola. *0730–2030*.
Nagerhole National Park (One day trip Somnathpur, Talkad and Shivasamudram).
Reservations : KSTDC counter in the Hotel Mayura Hoysala Complex, J L B Road *(Tel 236562)*.
KSTDC Information Counter, City Railway Station *(Tel 30719)*.

Kaveri Emporium, Sayyaji Rao Road.
Tickets are also available through authorised selling agents and travel agencies. All tours start and terminate at the KSTDC counter, Hotel Maurya Hoysala on J B L Road unless otherwise mentioned.

Museums and Libraries

Since several educational and research centres are located in Mysore there is no dearth of specialised research libraries covering a range of fields. Although there are not many museums, Mysore can nevertheless boast of one large museum and three smaller, specialised ones.

Chamarajendra Art Gallery A1 186

Chamarajendra Art Gallery in the Jagan Mohan Palace is essentially an exhibition of the paintings of the artist Ravi Verma. One of his famous pieces entitled 'Lady with a Lamp' is also exhibited here. The rest of the Jagan Mohan Palace contains assorted exhibits from the many palaces in the city.

Chamarajendra Art Gallery (Jagan Mohan Palace)

Of special interest are the carved ivory bric-a-brac, the weapons room, and a rich collection of musical instruments.

Rail Museum. See Gazetteer.

K A R P Museum D3 187

Karnataka's Mounted Company of Armed Reserve Police was originally H H Maharaja of Mysore's Bodyguard. The tiny museum located at the K A R P headquarters on Lalith Mahal Road has neat displays of uniforms, standards bearing the crest and colours of the bodyguard corp and photographs of exemplary men who served in it; *open 1000–1300* and *1500–1700.*

Folk Museum B1 184

The University of Mysore (Manasa Gangotri) contains an interesting representative collection of art, craft, costumes and other exhibits from all over Karnataka. Contact the University office in Crawford Hall.

The Palace Library A2 186

It is said that during the tumultuous reign of Tipu Sultan several manuscripts were destroyed when on his orders they were consigned to the flames for boiling 'kuli' or horsegram. Nevertheless the Palace Library is still one of the finest in the state with an excellent collection of books and manuscripts on philosophy and religion in particular, and several unpublished poems and treatises on various subjects in Kannada and Sanskrit. Contact the Secretary, Jagan Mohan Palace.

University of Mysore Library

This contains an excellent representative collection of over five lakh books and two lakh periodicals covering a wide range of subjects.

Oriental Research Institute D2 185

This is a treasure trove of rare Sanskrit and Kannada manuscripts numbering over 16,000 and about 20,000 printed vol umes. There is a special section which specialises in the research and publication of original texts on philosophy, law, medicine, astronomy and music, *Tel 23136.*

Library in the Central Food Technological Research Institute **D1 185**

Contact Mr Nair, *Tel 22660.*

Sri Ramakrishna Ashram Library **B1 168**

Contains mainly books on religion, philosophy, classics and Indian mythology; *open 1600–1800, Tel 22027.*

Art and Culture in Mysore

As the capital of the Mysore state and the seat of the Wodeyars who were generous patrons of art, Mysore was a mecca for men of literature, art, music and dance. However, Independence and the subsequent abolition of the privy purse put both patron and artist out of tune and Mysore's status as a cultural centre waned.

In September – October, however, Mysore recaptures its former glory. During Dussehra the city is drowned in colourful cultural festivities as music and dance performances by leading exponents are held in the grounds adjoining the palace. Fairs and exhibitions are also held in the Doddakere Maidan close to the palace for almost a month.

In recent years Mysore is being rediscovered as an ideal venue for cultural programmes. National and international troupes are beginning to put Mysore on their itinerary. Local newspapers carry advance information of when and where the shows are held, and tickets are usually also sold at the concerned auditoria and 'sabhas' (concert halls).

The Fine Arts College in the Manasa Gangotri conducts courses in classical dance, dance dramas, music, painting and handicraft. The Principal can be contacted for details.

The Chamarajendra Technical Institute on Sayyaji Rao Road run by the Government of Karnataka offers courses in

Dussehra Procession

painting, woodcutting, inlay work and sculpture. An exhibition of their work is on permanent display and individual orders can be placed with them, *Tel 23883*.

Theatre

Theatre is extremely popular in Mysore; there are several amateur groups and community organisations which put up shows from time to time. Theatre and drama are mostly in Kannada, with an occasional play in other Indian languages by members of various ethnic communities in the city. There are no indigenous English language theatre groups and no English plays.

Outstation artistes especially foreign musicians and bands on tour of India are brought to Mysore under the auspices of the Mysore Music Association. Contact the Secretary, Jagan Mohan Palace. Details of theatre and music performances appear in the evening daily 'The Star of Mysore'.

Auditoria

Ranga Mandira, Hunsur Road.
Visvesvaraya Hall (Institute of Engineers), J L Road.
Bal Bhavan, Bannimantap Extension.

Sports Club Auditorium, Lalith Mahal Road, *Tel 20743.*
Nada Brahma Sangeeta Sabha, J L Road (Contact Mr. Raja Rao, *Tel 31177).*
Chamarajendra Cultural Academy (auditorium in the Jagan Mohan Academy).

Entertainment

Mysore believes in the old adage 'early to bed and early to rise', consequently very few restaurants have live performers and dance floors. Entertainment is largely confined to cultural performances and, of course, the movies.

Sports

Cricket like everywhere else in India is very popular in Mysore and impromptu matches are held in every available open space. There are facilities for playing tennis, golf and other games; riding and yoga are other activities which may be enjoyed in the city.

Cricket
Cosmopolitan Club, Jubilee Road, *Tel 23881.*
Mysore Sports Club, Lalith Mahal Road, *Tel 20743.*

Riding
KARP Riding School, Lalith Mahal Road.

Swimming
University pool in Saraswatipuram.
Corporation pool on Chamaraja Double Road.

Hotels
Hotel Southern Star.
Lalith Mahal Palace Hotel offers a combined package of tennis and swimming facilities.

Tennis
Courts are restricted to members only. However, guests of members are allowed to use the facilities.
Cosmopolitan Club, Jubilee Road.
Mysore Tennis Club near the Law Courts.

Golf
The Mysore Golf Club (c/o the Race Club) has an 18 hole course on the race course. Non-members are allowed to play on payment of a 'greer fee'.

Dog Shows
The Mysore Kennel Club holds annual dog shows in October. The event attracts large crowds from outside the city, *Tel 52031*.

Shopping

More than anywhere else in India, Mysore offers a feast for the olfactory senses. Shops that sell wooden articles and agarbattis are imbued with the mingled fragrances of their waves, and create an atmosphere uniquely Mysorean. The city is probably the largest centre for the manufacture of incense sticks in India. Agarbattis in various fragrances and attars of rose, musk, jasmine, sandal wood and other fragrances are exported all over the world.

Mysore's craftspersons are famous for their woodwork—intricately carved pieces in teakwood, rosewood and sandalwood, ranging from little boxes to mammoth elephants. They are worth a trip to a handicrafts shop even if one doesn't intend to buy anything. Many of the pieces including furniture are delicately inlaid with ivory which create stunning designs and patterns.

Best shops Cauvery Arts and Crafts Emporium on Sayyaji Rao Road; Happy Handicrafts on Bangalore Road; Ganesh Industrial and Fine Arts on Dhanvanthri Road; Suryani Fine Arts on Dhanvanthri Road. There are several shops along Dhanvanthri Road and Irwin Road which sell handicrafts in the same price range as those in the Cauvery Emporium.

To complete this feast for the senses are the Mysore silk saris renowned for their texture and quality. The Karnataka Silk Industries Corporation (KSIC) silk weaving factory which was started in 1932 produces three types of pure silk saris—the crepe silk, soft silk and silk georgette. The difference lies in the warp and weft. The zari (gold thread) woven in traditional designs comes from Surat in Gujarat and consists of yarn plated with silver and then with gold. The metal content in the zari is about 33 per cent silver and 67 per cent gold which is why the price of the sari fluctuates with the price of gold. However, not all saris are with zari work. Printed saris in gorgeous shades and prints can be converted into dresses and other garments of one's choice. One can also buy material by the metre.

Best shops Showroom at KSIC factory on Madhwacharya Road; KSIC Showroom on Sayyaji Rao Road; Cauvery Arts and Crafts on Sayyaji Rao Road; Lakshmi Vilas on Sayyaji Rao Road; Bhojayya and Sons on Sayyaji Rao Road.

Silver jewellery in attractive designs and other silverware can be found on Ashoka Road which is lined with shops run by silversmiths. Ashoka Road is also well known for stainless steel articles.

Furnishing shops are largely concentrated on Devraj Urs Road. One can also find boutiques which sell readymade garments, linen and attractive items for the home.

Shops are usually open between *1000 and 1930* with a lunch break between *1330 and 1530*. The main shopping areas are Sayyaji Rao Road, Devraj Urs Road and Ashoka Road.

Eating out

Although Mysore would definitely not qualify as a gourmet's favourite city there are plenty of restaurants which serve reasonably good 'meals'—the standard south Indian vegetarian fare consisting of chapathi, rice, a variety of vegetables, dhal and curd, for a fixed sum. There are also several north Indian and some Chinese restaurants if one wants a change from the ever available 'meals'!

Mysore's contribution to south Indian cuisine is the 'set dosai', a thicker version of the ordinary dosai which is made from a fermented dough of ground rice and lentil. Crisp on one side and soft on the other this delicious dish can be eaten with 'sambar' (spiced lentils) and coconut 'chutney' (coconut ground with salt and spices).

The restaurants in the directory are listed under three categories: Expensive, Moderate and Inexpensive. The categories indicate the average price for a full meal for one, without liquor. In the more expensive restaurants tips of about 10 per cent of the bill are expected except where service charges are added.

Best shops Snacks and fruit juices are gaining popularity in Mysore. Bombay Juice Centre, Dhanvantri Road, (for fruit juices), Paras Restaurant, Sayyaji Rao Road (for snacks), Toot-C (for pizzas, burgers and pastries), Kalpaka, Dhanvantri Road (for juices, vegetable burgers and ice cream), Khatta Meetta Restaurant, Dhanvantri Road (for snacks), Nalpak, Devraj Urs Road (for south Indian snacks) and Bombay Tiffany's, Sayyaji Rao Road (for excellent snacks, especially samosas).

Very few restaurants have live bands and dance floors; one is more likely to find entertainment in the moderate and inexpensive restaurants where owners, patrons and waiters interact in easy camaraderie so typical of this friendly city.

Accommodation

Mysore offers one the choice of living in princely style in an erstwhile maharaja's palace (of which there are two) or more humbly in tourist lodges of which there are several. While the three and four star hotels offer such facilities as room service, attached restaurants and conference and banquet halls, the smaller hotels and lodges offer clean rooms, friendly service and close proximity to eating and shopping areas as inducements.

The hotels listed in the directory are under three categories :

Luxury (Rs 200 and upwards), Moderate (Rs 100 to Rs 200) and Budget (Rs 50 to Rs 100). The budget hotels far outnumber the moderate and luxury hotels and are popular with Indian and foreign tourists alike. Although standards vary, they are considered very good value for money. Most of them offer such amenities as attached baths, hot water and a highly individualised room service. A tip of a rupee or two a day will ensure that every need is taken care of, from bringing newspapers in the morning to fetching laundry and carrying dinner up to the room.

Most hotels insist on a *1200* check in/out, although the hotels in the budget category are more flexible about this rule. All hotels in general will install an extra bed to make a triple on request and the additional charge usually works out to about 25 per cent to 50 per cent extra on the normal tariff. Most hotels also include a service charge, sales tax and in the case of the larger hotels, luxury tax as well.

The railway retiring rooms offer alternative accommodation but can be used by railway passengers only. Accommodation here costs Rs 50 per bed in a double bedroom for 24 hours, and Rs 25 per bed in a dormitory for the same duration. (The rates are subject to change)

Travel

Travel to and from Mysore is largely routed through Bangalore to which it is well-connected by rail and bus. There are also bus and rail links to several satellite towns and certain cities in the bordering states.

AIR

The Indian Airlines office in Mysore will make bookings, if asked, on the several flights that they operate throughout the country. A recently established computer link-up has facilitated this process.

TRAIN

Besides the six express and three passenger trains shuttling between Bangalore and Mysore, there are several others linking Mysore to a few satellite towns. In most cases tickets are easily available and can be bought at the station on the day of the journey. Mysore also has a quota reserved in the overnight Madras Mail and also several other trains to various parts of the country that leave from Bangalore.
Enquiries, Reservation and **Cancellation** Mysore City Station, *Tel 20100.*

BUS

Buses are an extremely popular form of transport being more frequent and connecting a wider range of cities and towns than the railways. The suburban buses from the City Bus Stand on Albert Victor Road connect Mysore with towns within a short radius of the city. They are extremely convenient if one wants to go to Shrirangapattana, Somnathpur, Hassan (which can be used as a base for trips to Belur, Halebid, Shravanabelagola), Ooty (through the Bandipur and Mudumalai Game Sanctuaries), etc. The busy Inter-City Bus Stand on Church Road is a terminus for buses to and from cities both within and outside the state of Karnataka.

City Bus Stand, Albert Victor Road, *Tel 25019.*
Inter-City Bus Stand, Church Road, *Tel 20853.*

CARS AND VANS

Cars, vans and mini-buses can be hired from approved travel agencies and taxi operators. The ITDC and KSTDC also offer vehicles on hire. Different agencies offer different rates and schemes so it is necessary to enquire at a few agencies and select an offer which suits one best.

Picnics and Excursions

Bandipur Game Sanctuary

Once a game reserve of the Wodeyars' Bandipur, just 80 kms from Mysore on the Ooty road, is one of the major game sanctuaries in India. Separated from the Mudumalai Sanctuary in Tamil Nadu by the Moyer river it is an important precinct of the 'Project Tiger' dedicated to the conservation of these magnificent beasts. The sanctuary is also home for the bison, spotted deer, elephants, black panthers, leopards, bears and a host of other wild animals. Artificial salt licks and 'machans' or raised platforms help in getting a closer view. One can go around the sanctuary in forest jeeps or on elephant back. There are forest lodges for stay.

Season : Jan–Jun, Sep–Oct.

Accommodation : Contact Field Director, Project Tiger, Government House Complex, Irwin Road, *Tel 20901.*

Regular buses from the CBS to Bandipur.

Gomatagiri

Twentyfive kilometres from Mysore on the Mysore–Mercara Road and not far from the Cauvery river is this small Jain pilgrim spot earlier called Shravanaghutta. The four metre black stone statue of Bahubali though not as awe-inspiring as the one in Shravanabelagola, does have dignity and a strange arresting charm.

There is a Jain dharmashala run by the Sri Gomatagiri Kshetra Seva Samithi.

Kakanakote

Elephants from Karnataka prized for their size and strength were once trapped in this forest by the Khedda method which involved herding and lassoing them in large numbers at a time by skilled tribesmen. Khedda operations are now few and far between and one can see large herds of elephants peacefully grazing here. The Kabini river flows through the forest; the forest and river combination has made Kakana kote a popular tourist spot. Accommodation is available in a Forest Lodge and a Travellers Bungalow.

The Jungle Lodge and Resorts Ltd provides boarding, lodging and wildlife viewing from jeeps, elephant-back, and corracles (basket shaped boats made of cane and lined with tar paulin or buffalo hide) which glide silently over the water.

Season : *Sep–Jun.*

For accommodation at the Tourist Bunglow and Jungle Lodge and Resorts Ltd contact: Government of Karnataka Regional Tourist Office, Old Exhibition Bldg, Irwin Road, *Tel 22096.*

Melkote **B3 130**

Melkote, meaning high or superior fort, is 64 km from Mysore. It was an important centre for learning since the early twelfth century when the Vaishnava sage Ramanujacharya sought shelter here from the persecution of a Chola king. It is now a principal seat of the Vaishnavas (followers of Vishnu). The rocky Yadugiri Hills is surmounted by the famous Narasimha temple which is supposed to have a very valuble collection of jewels. Equally valuble is the private library of the Swamigal (head) of Melkote, now part of the Academy for Sanskrit Research, which has several unpublished works in Sanskrit, Tamil, philosophy, logic, rhetoric, maths, astronomy, etc. The popular Vairamudi festival (crowning the ruling Vaishnava deity with a diamond studded crown) in April attracts many devotees from various parts of south India. There are choultries available for stay and a regular bus service operates from Mysore.

Nagamangala **B3 130**

It is about 80 km from Mysore and is well known for its many interesting temples, the most important being the Saumya Kesava temple which was built in the Hoysala style of architecture. Metal work is a flourishing industry here and several of the beautiful idols in its temples were said to have been cast here.

There are choultries available for stay.

Nagarhole National Park **B3 130**

This forest 93 km from Mysore covers an area of 570 sq km. It is home to the bison, sloth bear, elephants and a variety of other wildlife.

For accommodation and **transport** to the National Park contact: Asst Conservator of Forests, Wildlife Preservation, Chamarajendra Circle, *Tel 21159.*

Nanjangud

A temple town 24 km from Mysore off the Ooty road, it is famous for its variety of temples of which the Nanjandeshwara is the most famous. A popular car festival is held for three days every year at the end of March.

Regular buses operate from Mysore.

Ranganathittu Bird Sanctuary **B3 130**

A delightful spot for birdwatchers, Ranganathittu is 16 km from Mysore on the way to Shrirangapattana and consists of several islets in the River Cauvery. A boat ride around the islets offers a wonderful view of herons, ibis, storks, cormorants and other water birds.

Season : May–Nov.

Buses from Mysore to Shrirangapattna will stop here on request. There are taxis from Shrirangapattana to Ranganathittu.

Shivasamudram C3 131

An island town 80 km from Mysore, Shivasamudram is known for its beautiful twin waterfalls, the Gaganachukki and the Bharachukki, which plunge about 60m down. It is magnificent in the rainy season and is a picturesque spot during the dry season when the falls consist of several silvery streams cascading down.

There is a regular bus service from Mysore.

Talkad C3 131

According to tradition, Talkad, 45 km from Mysore, was named after two brothers Tala and Kadu who attained enlightenment here. Talkad was once the capital of the Ganga dynasty (330-500 A.D.) but the old city of Talkad is now completely buried under sand dunes. According to a legend a conquering ruler tried to force his attentions on the virtuous wife of another man. Her curse turned Talkad into a desert, the Malangi river into a whirlpool and left the ruler heirless. The tops of some of the structures are visible, however, and chief of these is the Kirthinarayana temple built by Vishnuvardhana of the Hoysala dynasty to commemorate his victory over the Cholas in 1117 A.D. Once in about twelve years the temple is laboriously uncovered for the performance of 'Panchalinga Darshan', but the sand soon reclaims it.
There are buses from Mysore.

Tourist Spots near Mysore

Krishnarajasagar Dam B3 130

Northwest of Mysore at the confluence of the Cauvery, Hemvati and Lakshmanathirta rivers is the Krishnarajasagar (KR) dam, completed in 1932 and named after Krishnaraja Wodeyar IV. Earlier efforts at building a dam across the confluence including one by Tipu Sultan had come to naught. The present dam 2606m long and constructed entirely in stone without any cement forms a 130 sq km lake on one side. On the other side the immensely popular Brindavan Gardens

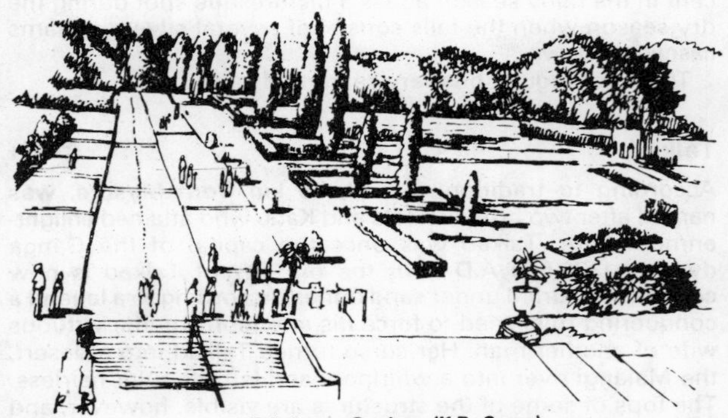

Brindavan Gardens (K.R. Sagar)

stretch out in terraces along the length of the dam. Beautifully laid out flower beds and well-maintained lawns are complemented by innumerable pools and fountains. At night the gardens are transformed into a kind of fairyland when the concealed lights near the flower beds and fountains are turned on and add a new dimension to the gardens.

Somnathpur **C3 131**

In a quiet little village, 14 km east of Mysore on the left bank of the Cauvery river is the third famous Hoysala temple, the Prasanna Chenna Kesava. Both the village and the temple owe their existence to Soma, an important official of royal birth who lived during the reign of King Narasimha III.

Built in 1268 A.D. the Prasanna Chenna Kesava is similar to the Chenna Kesava in Belur and the Hoysaleswara in Halebid in architecture and sculpture. The temple is situated in the middle of a courtyard which is ringed with an open hall containing 64 cells. The plinth, supported at the angles by miniature stone elephants, adds a distinct touch of individuality to the temple. Unlike the other two temples, however, the Prasanna Chenna Kesava is a 'trikutachala' or three-celled temple with the main shrine dedicated to Kesava, an aspect of Vishnu. All three cells are surmounted by individual 'vimanas' or towers, elegantly carved and identical in design. This frontage often serves as a popular model for etchings on the gold and silver caskets made in the area.

On the exterior walls of the temple is a row of spirited renditions of important incidents in the epics, the *Ramayana* and the *Mahabharata*. A whimsical touch added by the sculptor are the half-closed doors indicating the end of a chapter! The other rows contain sculptures of richly caprisoned elephants, charging horsemen, scrollwork, mythological beasts and swans, and finally columns with figures in between.The ceiling panels inside match the intricacy of the carvings outside with perforated screens providing light.

Shrirangapattana **B3 130**

Tipu Sultan's erstwhile island capital, Shrirangapattana, is surrounded by the Cauvery which forks out and flows around it. The town takes its name from Sri Ranganathaswamy, the presiding deity who is enshrined in one of the oldest Dravidian temples in the state. It was built in 1120 A.D. by Udayaditya, brother of Vishnuvardhana the Hoysala king. A fort was built in 1454 after Shrirangapattana passed into the hands of the Vijayanagar kings; this was considerably enlarged and fortified in the eighteenth century and stands strong even today.

The temple itself was first built in 894 A.D. and was expanded during the reign of the Hoysalas; the 'navaranga' was built around 1454 by the Vijayanagar kings. Two pillars in front of the inner entrance of the temple are decorated with carvings of Vishnu in his twentyfour 'murtis' or forms. In a legend originating from the Puranas, Ranganatha (another name for Vishnu) settled here at the request of Cauvery, the river goddess. The idol itself is worth seeing: a colossal figure of Ranganatha reclining on Adisesha, the seven-headed serpent. The Goddess Cauvery is seated at his feet holding a lotus in her hand. Some of the silver vessels used by the temple for its rituals were gifts from Tipu Sultan who also donated a sword and worshipped at the temple from outside. Tipu who had a Hindu wife never sat down to a meal until he heard the temple bell.

In the intervals when he was not fighting the British, Tipu built his pleasure palaces. The one at Shrirangapattana called the Daria Daulat Bagh (Garden of the Wealth of the Sea) was built in 1784. Set in large, manicured grounds the Daria Daulat Bagh, like the palace in Bangalore, is built mainly in

Daria Daulat

wood and its simple wooden facade is unusually modest for a royal residence. The chief features of this Saracenic style building are the paintings which decorate every inch of the west wall including the narrow stair-walls and doors. On the west wall are large murals graphically describing Tipu's victory over Colonel Baillie's army in Kancheepuram in 1780. A little time spent here will reveal delightful details : Tipu on horseback unconcernedly smelling a bouquet of flowers while surrounded by the mayhem of the battle; moustaches on all French soldiers under Tipu to distinguish them from the British who were invariably clean shaven except for the traditional mutton-chop whiskers.

A small but interesting museum on Tipu is housed in the building.

The main entrance to the fort rebuilt by Tipu Sultan in 1791 was through the Elephant Gate in the south. Within the walls was Tipu's main palace of which nothing remains. However, the Water Gate through which the British breached the fort in 1799 can still be seen as also the spot where Tipu was killed while bravely fighting the oncoming British army. Tipu's favourite mosque, the white painted Juma Masjid with its unusually small dome and two predominant towers, is also an interesting landmark.

About one kilometre away at the eastern end of the island is the Gumbaz built by Tipu Sultan as a mausoleum for his parents. Thirtysix black hornblende pillars (polished regularly

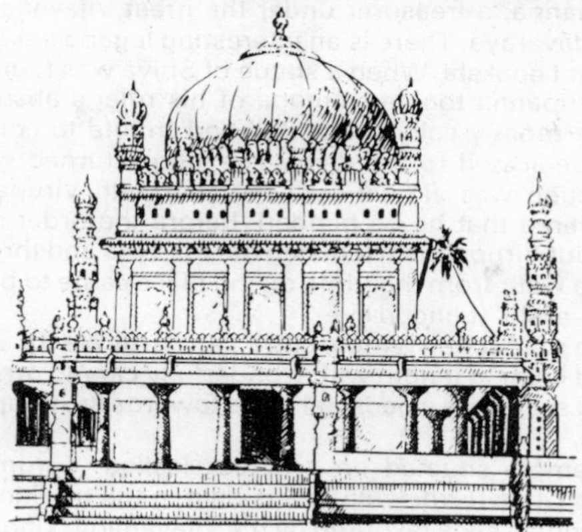
The Gumbaz

with coconut oil to maintain their shine) support a cream coloured square structure surmounted by a bulbous dome, both surrounded by low parapets with miniature minarets at the four corners and decorated with intricate plaster work. The interior is painted with the tiger stripe which Tipu favoured for his military uniforms. The ebony double doors with ivory inlay echo the colour scheme of the exterior.

Hoggenakkal – the 'smoking rock'

The Cauvery at Hoggenakkal is fascinating. It is considered sacred at Hoggenakkal. Coracles are ideal for navigating the rock-strewn river at Hoggenakkal. The boats move in huge circular motion and can be hired. The landscape is full of misshapen ledges and furrows. It is a place of vintage natural beauty, uncongested, undiscovered and unspoilt.

Lepakshi

C2 131

Although not strictly within the borders of Karnataka, Lepakshi is included here because of its proximity to and easy accessibility from Bangalore. Lepakshi is connected by bus with Bangalore and there is a rail link between Bangalore and

Hindupur, 17 km from Lepakshi. There are regular buses from Hindupur to Hyderabad, Bangalore and Tirupathi.

There is a temple of Veerabhadra (an aspect of Shiva) built by Virupanna, a treasurer under the great Vijayanagar king Krishnadevaraya. There is an interesting legend linked to this temple at Lepakshi. When a statue of Shiva was found at this spot, Virupanna took advantage of his ruler's absence and used the money collected as tax and tribute to construct a temple dedicated to the deity. The king returned when the construction was almost over. Furious with Virupanna the king ordered that he be blinded. Before the order could be carried out Virupanna wrenched out his eyes and threw them against a wall; from that time on the place came to be known as 'Lepa-akshi' (blinded eye).

On the road to the temple sits a very large Nandi. It is 6.5m high and 4.8m in length with wonderfully carved ornamentation, and seated on a pedestal looks towards the temple in the distance.

The temple situated on a hillock (called 'Kurumasalem' (because of its tortoise-shape) is built in the traditional opulent Dravidian style favoured by the Vijayanagar kings. Within the complex are several smaller structures like the pillared verandahs meant for camping devotees, the enormous statue of Ganesha carved out of the hillface, and the 6.5m black granite nagalingam, encircled and protected by a giant nine-headed naga (cobra).

Within the enclosure is the kalyana mantapa, roofless in its unfinished state. The carvings on the pillars depict the marriage of Shiva and Parvati. An intricate pattern of men with shared heads and multiple bodies can be seen. Amongst several other breathtaking carvings a cow, seemingly alive, adopts three perfectly bovine postures with her three heads.

Possibly the most famous part of the temple is the Natya Mantap (Dance Hall) which has sixtysix pillars carved with lifesize figures of Brahma, Nataraja (dancing Shiva) and others dancing or playing various musical instruments. The incredibly beautiful paintings executed in rich, earthy colours (derived from vegetable and other natural dyes) on either side of the central portion of the ceiling depict ancient fables.

The 'floating pillar' in this hall, hanging suspended off the floor, is an engineering marvel. Legends say that at the beginning of this century an English engineer had the pillar shifted by using a crowbar at its base. When the pillar moved so did all the other bases, which are still slightly askew, counterpoised by the pillar.

The sanctum - sanctorum contains images of Veerabhadra (the raging Shiva) and Durga, an awesome aspect of Parvati. But there is also a Shivalinga and a shrine dedicated to Vishnu. In a curious juxtaposition the Linga is set in the lotus seat of Vishnu while the latter sits amidst the coils of a naga. According to some this temple symbolises the oneness of god and worship, and if symbol is pitted against symbol the rage of Shiva will destroy this 'divisive evil'.
Tourist Rest House, Lepakshi. Contact District Public Relations Officer, Ananthpur, *Tel 515331.*

General Information

Ambulance On call 24 hrs, *Tel 102*

Bangalore

Also at fixed timings, generally *0900–1800* at:
Bowring and Lady Curzon Hospital, *Tel 570782/561362*
St John's Hospital, *Tel 530724*
St Martha's Hospital, *Tel 215081*
St Philomina's Hospital, *Tel 577046*
Vani Vilas Hospital, *Tel 608887*
Victoria Hospital, *Tel 606575*
City Corporation Ambulance, *Tel 230789*
K C General Hospital, *Tel 361791*
Civil Corporation Ambulance, *Tel 571488*

Mysore

Basappa Memorial Hospital
K R Hospital, *Tel 20252*
Holdsworth Memorial Hospital (Mission Hospital), *Tel 21650*
Anglo-American Hospital, *Tel 21333*

Chemists See Directory of Services.

Climate and Clothing Bangalore's pleasant climate (min. 20°C max. 35°C) has long been a major attraction with tourists. A tolerable summer from Feb-May (min. 20°C max. 35°C) and a moderate monsoon comprising short, sharp showers have ensured that the tourist season in Bangalore occurs all the year round. The crisp and pleasant winter (min 14°C max 28°C) from Nov – Jan is the best season to visit Bangalore.

Cottons and light silks are ideal wear for Banglaore. Light woollens are recommended for the winter, especially at nights, and if you plan to visit some south Indian hill stations. None of the hotels specify dress regulations.

Climate and Clothing Although on a slightly lower elevation (770 m) than Bangalore (920 m) Mysore too enjoys a very equable climate. Summer from Mar-Jun (min 20°C max 35°C) is followed by a moderate (86 cm) monsoon season which lasts from Jun-Nov. Occasional cloudy skies and sudden drops in temperature are typical of this period. Winter months from Dec-Feb are the most pleasant (min 14°C max 28°C). Despite the changes in seasons, the typical Mysore weather is clear, crisp and invigorating.

Cottons and light silks are ideal wear for Mysore. Light woollens are recommended for the winter, especially at night, and if one plans to spend a few days in some south Indian hill station.

Currency and Banks Hundred paise make one Indian rupee (Re, Rs) and currency rates are issued in denominations of 1, 2, 5, 10, 20, 50 and 100 (US$ 1 = Rs 34 and UK£ 1 = Rs 50 approximately). Coins come in denominations of 5, 10, 20, (light aluminium) 25, 50, Rs 1, Rs 2 (both are more or less the same shape and size, so watch out) and Rs 5 (silver nickel).

All tourists, including Indian nationals residing abroad, are required to pay hotel bills in convertible foreign currencies (US $, £, DM etc.)

Foreign exchange in excess of US $ 1000 or its equivalent must be declared on the Currency Declaration Form on arrival. Foreign currency upto the amount imported and declared on the CDF may be taken out of India on departure. It is illegal to bring in or take out Indian currency.

All money (drafts, bills, traveller's cheques etc.) should be changed only through authorised banks and money changers (listed in the Directory) and the receipt retained to reconvert unused Indian rupees. Changing money through unauthorised persons is illegal. The airport and some deluxe hotels have money changers. International credit cards are accepted only at the larger hotels, shops and stores.

Electricity Power is generated at 220V 50 cycles AC. American appliances (110V 60 cycles) require a transformer. Frequent voltage fluctuations and power cuts especially in summer make the use of a voltage stabilizer essential.

Foreigners Registration Office The Commissioner of Police, Infantry Road, is the Foreigners Registration Authority, *Tel 266242*.

Foreign Travel Tax (Rs. 300) is payable by all passengers travelling to any place outside India from an airport/seaport, and Rs. 150 to neighbouring countries of Afghanistan, Bhutan, Bangladesh, Burma, Nepal, Pakistan, Sri Lanka and Maldives.

Health Make it a rule to drink only boiled or otherwise treated water. When in doubt opt for piping hot tea or coffee, bottled aerated drinks of reputed manufacture (Thums Up, Limca, Gold Spot, Leher Pepsi, 7 Up etc) or mineral water available in disposable plastic bottles at large departmental stores and chemists. You can also choose from a wide variety of fruit juices and milk shakes available in tetrapacks. Cooked, fresh, hot food is usually safe to consume but most Indian food tends to be spicy. Avoid raw salads and fruits.

OTC and prescription drugs and anti-malarial pills are available at chemists.

Cholera and typhoid inoculation are recommended. A valid international certificate of vaccination against yellow fever is required for all, including infants, who have passed through areas considered endemic (Latin America, Africa). Visitors without these certificates are subject to quarantine for a minimum period of six days. Cholera, typhoid and other inoculations are available at all govt. hospitals and dispensaries.

Casualty and emergency wards in govt. and some private hospitals are open 24 hrs. Out patient Departments (OPD), general wards and private rooms are also available. Only govt. hospitals accept cases with medico-legal implications (accidents, burns, etc.). Many hotels have a doctor on call.

Holidays Sunday is the weekly holiday for most commercial establishments. Most offices close on Saturday or work half day. All govt. offices work *0930–1730* Mon–Fri. Closed on Sat and Sun. In addition to the four national holidays (Jan 26–Republic Day, May 1–May Day, Aug 15–Independence Day, Oct 2–Gandhi Jayanthi), establishments are closed on festival days and gazetted holidays which are declared at the beginning of each year and which vary from state to state. Since Indian festivals are determined by the lunar calender, they also vary from year to year.

Banks work *1030–1430* Mon-Fri and *1030–1230* on Sat. Most banks in commercial areas are closed on Sun. Banks in Residential areas are closed on Mon and open on Sun. Shops are open from *1000–2000* with a longish lunch break between *1330–1500* though many smaller shops work without a break. Some Shops close on Fri *(1200–1600)* to facilitate Muslims to offer prayers.

'Annual events' provide a rough idea of festival days.

Liquor and Drugs Prohibition is not in force in Karnataka. There are several pubs in the city which offer a wide variety of liquor and bottled and draught beer as well. Many restaurants also have a bar attached.

Possession of drugs (opium, hashish, marijuana, etc.) is illegal.

Measurement The metric system has been adopted officially, but you may occasionally come across use of the imperial measure.

Police Traffic policemen in Bangalore, identified by khaki and white uniforms and white stetson-style hats understand enough of English and Hindi to be of help. The Bangalore traffic policemen are usually helpful and effective. All police stations (PS on maps) register complaints and may be approached for help. However, contact the police department only in the case of an emergency; approach the Govt. of India Tourist office or Karnataka State Tourist office for any other help. Dial *100* in an emergency. The Police Commissioner's office is on Infantry Road, Bangalore-1, *Tel 264501.*

In Mysore too, traffic policemen, identified by their khaki and white uniform and white hats are usually helpful. Approach the Tourist Bureau, Dept. of Tourism, Govt. of Karnataka or Karnataka State Tourism Development Corporation for any other help. Dial *100* for emergencies. The office of the Deputy Inspector General of Police is in Jalapuri (Gandhinagar), *Tel 22200.*

Postal Services Most post offices (PO on maps) in Bangalore are open on Sat *0930–1730.* The General Post Office (GPO), Raj Bhavan Road, *Tel 266772* is open 24 hours all days of the week and provides Post Restante facilities. Postage stamps are sold at post offices and mobile post office vans. Postal rates in India vary according to weight (2.00 for envelopes upto 20 gms, 0.75 p. for inland letter forms and 0.25 p. for post cards). Postal rates for foreign mails vary depending on the weight and destination. The postal clerk will weigh the letter and specify the required postage. Parcels must not be sealed but secured so that they can be easily opened. A customs declaration form (CDF) has to be filled in for overseas parcels.

A 'Speedpost' service is available at the GPO, HPO and some of the larger PO's, which ensures 24-hour delivery, *Tel 200404.*

The General Post Office (GPO) in Mysore on Ashoka Road is open until *2000* hrs, and is also open on Sundays, *Tel 20052.*

Telegrams In Bangalore ordinary and express telegrams can be sent from all main post offices and all post and telegraph offices during working hours. Telegrams may also be sent from the Central Telegraph Office, Raj Bhavan Road, open 24 hours. The message must be written on a form available at the counter; rates are charged per word.

In Mysore telegrams may also be sent from the Central Telegraph Office, Sayyaji Rao Road, *Tel 20301*.

Telephone Public call office (PCO) for local calls are available in all post offices, air and rail terminals and markets in Bangalore. Pay phones take Re 1 coins only. STD (Subscriber Trunk Dialling) calls to cities in India may be made from the larger post offices, air and rail terminals and a number of STD booths open 24 hours. Several shops permit the use of their telephones for local calls and usually charge Rs 2 per call. Automatic STD is available to most cities in India and most countries abroad. STD charges are quarter the normal rate between *2200–0600* and half the normal rate between *1700* and *2200* on weekdays, 24 hours on Sunday and national holidays. Ordinary, urgent and lightning calls may be booked from all the main post and telegraph offices during normal working hours. The GPO offers telex facilities upon payment of the required fee.

Contact Directory Enquiries, *Tel 197 or 200197* for telephone information, new telephone numbers or change in telephone numbers.

In Mysore there are several manned telephone booths all over the city.

Time The Indian Standard Time (IST) is about five and a half hours ahead of Greenwich Mean Time, ten hours ahead of the American Eastern Standard Time (New York), one hour behind Australian Eastern Standard Time and three hours behind the Japanese Standard Time verification (Tokyo). Dial *174* for IST.

Tipping It is not customary to tip auto and taxi drivers. Where service charges are not added to hotel and restaurant bills, tip about 10 per cent of the bill. An additional tip is usually expected even where a service charge is included. In small establishments and for special services rendered, tip from one rupee upwards.

Visa Extension Contact Foreigners Regional Registration Office.

Worship Important places of Christian, Hindu, Jain, Muslim, Sikh and Zoroastrian worship are listed in the Directory of Services.

Directory of Services – Bangalore

ACCOMMODATION

Expensive – Rs 1000 upwards
Moderate – Rs 500 – Rs 1000
Budget – Rs 100 – Rs 500

EXPENSIVE

Ashok Hotel, High grounds, *Tel 269462/3*
Holiday Inn, 28 Sankey Road, *Tel 267931/269451*
Taj Residency, 14 M G Road, *Tel 584444*
The Oberoi, 37/39 M G Road, *Tel 585858.*
West End Hotel, Race Course Road, *Tel 264191*
Windsor Manor, 25 Sankey Road, *Tel 269898*

MODERATE

Airlines Hotel, Lavelle Cross Road, *Tel 573783*
Bangalore International, Highlands, *Tel 268011/263012/268013*
Cauvery Continental, 11/37 Cunningham Road, *Tel 266968*
Curzon Court, 10 Brigade Road, *Tel 581698/582997*
Chalukya Hotel, 17 Museum Road, *Tel 577461*
Gateway Hotel, Residency Road, *Tel 584545*
Gautam Hotel, 44 Race Course Road, *Tel 265055*
Harsha, 11 Venkataswamy Naidu Road, *Tel 565566*
Hotel Nahar Heritage, 14 St Mark's Road, *Tel 213233/215976*
Luciya International, 6 OTC Road, *Tel 224148*
New Victoria, 47/48, 25 Residency Road, *Tel 571738*
Nilgiris Nest, 11 Brigade Road, *Tel 577501*
Rama, Lavelle Road, *Tel 213321*
Ramanashree Comforts, Richmond circle, *Tel 235250/225152*
Woodlands Hotel, 5 Sampige Tank Road, *Tel 236153*
Victoria Hotel, Opp. Maya Hall, *Tel 584076*

BUDGET

Ajanta Hotel, 22-A, M G Road, *Tel 573321*
Akshaya, 10 Sampige Tank Road, *Tel 221563/238296*
Blue Fox Hotel, 80 M G Road, *Tel 587608*
Bombay Anand Bhavan, 10 Grant Road, *Tel 214581*
Brindavan Hotel, 40 M G Road, *Tel 57321*
Chandravihar, Avenue Road (Near City Market), *Tel 224146*
Delhi Bhavan Lodge, 387 Avenue Road, *Tel 75049*
Ganesha Lodge, 14 Subedar Chatram Road, *Tel 364581*
Geo Hotel, 11 Devanga Sangha Hostel Road (Near Hudson Circle), *Tel 221583*
Grand Ishagia Hotel, 96 Police Road, *Tel 73502*
Hotel Gangotri, Seshadripuram, *Tel 363199*
Highlands, 9 Race Course Road, Madhava Nagar, *Tel 269235*
Janpath Hotel, 11/12 Albert Victor Road (Behind Bangalore Medical College), *Tel 601889*
Kamat Lodge, 98 Kilari Road, *Tel 24591*
Kamadhenu, Trinity Church Circle, M G Road, *Tel 574451*
Laxmi Hotel, 11 Ist Cross, Gandhinagar, *Tel 267971/269511*
Nataraj Hotel, 9 Residency Road (Richmond Circle), *Tel 578846*
Rainbow Hotel, 2/114 Narasimha Raja Road, *Tel 602235*
Raj Hotel, BVK Iyengar Road, *Tel 24183*
Sandya Lodge, 17 Subedar Chatram Road, *Tel 747078*
Santosh Hotel 5th Cross, Gandhinagar, *268806*
Sri Ramakrishna Lodge, S. Chatram Road, *Tel 263041*
Sudarshan Lodge, 7 Ramakrishnapuram, S. Chatram Road, *Tel 27709/27792*
Sudha Lodge, 6 Cottonpet Main Road, *Tel 605420*
Suprabhata (Lodge), Sri Krishna Complex, Anand Rao Circle, 32, Sheshadri Road, *Tel 79466/70213*
Swagath Hotel, Hospital Road (Balepet Cross), *Tel 70007/70826*
Tourist Hotel, Race Course Road, *Tel 262381*

(The rates are subject to change from time to time)

OTHERS

Railway Retiring Rooms, *Tel 29444*
Students Christian Movement, 29 CSI Compound, 2nd Cross, *Tel 223761*
Youth Hostel, (Off) Bramha Samaj Bldg., Oblappa, Gandhinagar, *Tel 601151*
YMCA, (for families) Nrupatunga Road, *Tel 211848*
YMCA, Nrupatunga Road, *Tel 212228*

AIRLINES

Air India, Unity Buildings Road, *Tel 224143*
British Airways, 33/1, Cunningham Road-52, *Tel 214915*

Cathay Pacific Airways, West End Hotel compound, Race Course-1, *Tel 26974*
Indian Airlines, Cauvery Bhavan, Karnataka Housing Board Bldg., Kempe Gowda Road, *Tel 214433*
Japan Airlines, B-2 Devata Plaza, Residency Road-25, *Tel 575416*
Kuwait Airways, 3/4 N Block, Unity Building, J C Road-27, *Tel 224513*
Lufthansa Airlines, Unity Building, J C Road-27, *Tel 564791*
Vayudoot GSA, KSTDC, Badami House, N R Square, *Tel 29769*

BANKS

Monday to Friday 1030 to 1430 hrs, Saturday 1030 to 1230 hrs.

Allahabad Bank, 2 Kempegowda Road, *Tel 262064*
Andhra Bank, Narasimharaja Road, *Tel 222607*
Bank of Baroda, 72 M G Road, *Tel 587909*
Bank of India, 49 St Mark's Road, *Tel 212795*
Bank of Madura, 394-6 Avenue Road, *Tel 75994*
Bank of Maharashtra, 190 Brigade Road, *Tel 588592*
Canara Bank, Overseas Branch, *Tel 584320*
Central Bank of India, Kempegowda Road, *Tel 73096*
Corporation Bank, 114 M G Road, *Tel 587940/588435*
Grindlays Bank, Unity Bldg., J C Road, *Tel 224463*
Indian Bank, 44/45 Residency Road, *Tel 582309*
Indian Overseas Bank, 10/1 Palace Road, Vasant Nagar, *Tel 266287*
Punjab National Bank, Big City Branch, *Tel 221093*
Punjab National Bank, Cantt. Branch, *Tel 563078*
State Bank of India, City Branch, *Tel 236701*
State Bank of India, Church Street, *Tel 588980, 588312*
State Bank of Mysore, 12/3 J C Road, *Tel 224675*

CHEMISTS

Arya Vaidya Pharmacy (Coimbatore), 5 Queens Road, *Tel 260916*
Al Siddique Pharma Centre, 1/1 N R Road, *Tel 605491* (24 hrs service)
Cash Pharmacy, 2 St Mark's Road, *Tel 210713*
Chetak Pharmacy, Devata Plaza Basement, 131/132 Residency Road, *Tel 212449*
Cavalry Chemists, 249 Cavalry Road, *Tel 570033*
Deepak Drug House, 12 Cubbonpet, *Tel 210447* (24 hrs service)
Janata Bazaar, Inside Victoria Hospital, *Tel 606575* (24 hrs service)
Mekhri Medical Shop, Opp. Vanivilas Hospital (24 hrs), *Tel 628034*
Srinivasa Medical Supplies, 18 Hospital Road, *Tel 265030*

CINEMAS

Abhinay, 3 BVK Iyengar Road (Hindi, Kannada), *Tel 27019/72029*
Apsara, city market square (Hindi films), *Tel 604935*
Blu Diamond/Blu Moon, M G Road (English films), *Tel BD - 587099, BM - 576537*
Galaxy, 43 Residency Road (English films), *Tel 582205*

Kalpana, Kempe Gowda Road (English films), *Tel 71494*
Kino, 19/20 Subedar Chatram Road (Tamil), *Tel 363907*
Lavanya, 11 St John's Road (Tamil), *Tel 572596*
Lido, Old Madras Road (Hindi), *Tel 571866*
Majestic, Kempe Gowda Circle (Telugu), *Tel 28905*
Navarang, 3rd Block, Rajajinagar (Kannada), *Tel 324186*
Nartaki, 25/26 Kempe Gowda Road (Hindi, Kannada), *Tel 258293*
Pallavi, 20 Sampige Tank Road (Telugu, Tamil), *Tel 223191*
Plaza, M G Road (English), *Tel 587682*
Prasanna, 92 Magadi Road (Kannada), *Tel 354759*
Rex, 12-13 Brigade Road (English), *Tel 587350*
Sangeetha, 41 Central Street (Tamil), *Tel 564098*
Santosh, K G Road (Hindi, Kannada), *Tel 75344*
Shankarnag, M G Road (English), Tel 585988
Tribhuvan, Kailash, Gandhinagar (English, Hindi), *Tel 261101*
Triveni, Kempegowda (Kannada), *Tel 71244*

HOSPITALS

Al Ameen Medical Trust, *Tel 260882*
Baptist Hospital, Bellary Road, *Tel 330321*
Bowring and Lady Curzon Hospital, Hospital Road, *Tel 561362*
Cancer Institute, *Tel 642061*
Central Laprosarium, Magadi Road, *Tel 350239*
Church of South India Hospital, Col. Hill Road, *Tel 571103/566256*
Chinmaya Mission Hospital, Indiranagar, *Tel 583040*
Dental College Hospital, Fort, *Tel 565053*
ESI Hospital, II Block, Rajajinagar, *Tel 324112*
ESI Hospital, Indiranagar, *Tel 566994*
HSIS Ghosha Hospital, Tasker Town, *Tel 566529*
Isolation Hospital, Bannamangalam, Old Madras Road, *Tel 571258*
Jayadeva Institute of Cardiology, Victoria Hospital, *Tel 601094/608677*
K C Central Hospital, 5th Cross, Malleswaram, *Tel 361771*
KIDWAI Memorial Institute of Oncology, Hosur Road, *Tel 605915/642061*
Lady Willingdon Tuberculosis Clinic and Dispensary, *Tel 267093*
Mallya–Apollo Hospital, *Tel 217979*
Manipal Hospital, *Tel 566791*
Minto Ophthalmic Hospital, Tipu Sultan Palace Road, *Tel 608092*
M S Ramaiah Medical Teaching Hospital, Gokul Extn., *Tel 363476/361515*
National Institute of Mental & Neuro Sciences, Hosur Road, *Tel 641256/642121*
Sanjay Gandhi Accident and Rehabilitation Hospital IV-T Block, Jayanagar, *Tel 643402*
SDS Sanatorium, Hosur Road, *Tel 632634*
Sindhi Charitable Trust Hospital, Sampangiramnagar, *Tel 221854/237117*
Sri Jayachamarajendra Institute of Indian Medicine, Seshadri Road, *Tel 72848*

St John's Medical College Hospital, Sarjapur Road, *Tel 530724/563185*
St Martha's Hospital, Nrupathunga Road, *Tel 215081*
St Philomena's Hospital, Nilasandra Road, *Tel 577046*
St. Theresa's Hospital, Ist Block Rajajinagar, *Tel 320432*
T B Sanatorium, Binnamangalam, Old Madras Road, *Tel 581245*
Vanivilas Hospital (for Women and Children), Sri Krishnarajendra Road, *Tel 608887*
Victoria Hospital, *606575*
Wochardt Hospital & Heart Institute, *Tel 261037*

INDIAN MEDICINE

Institute of Naturopathy and Yogic Sciences, 16 Tumkur Road, *Tel 394926*
Nature Cure Hospital, 29th Main Road, 3rd Block, *Tel 605945*

VETERINARY

Veterinary Hospital, Mysore Road, *Tel 600985*
Veterinary Hospital, Queen's Road, *Tel 266575*
SPCA Mobile Clinic, Queen's Statue Circle, *Tel 564038/331181*

RESTAURANTS

Expensive – Rs 75 and above
Moderate – between Rs 25 and Rs 75
Inexpensive – below Rs 25
Cuisine : South Indian Vegetarian (SVg), Non-Vegetarian (NVg), Vegetarian (Vg), Mughalai (M), Tandoori (T), Chinese (Ch), Continental (Cont), Mixed-Continental, Chinese, Mughalai (Mx)

EXPENSIVE

Bankura Punjabi Restaurant, St Mark's Road.
Blue Fox (Mx), 80 M G Road, *Tel 587608*
Caesar's (Mx), Mahalakshmi Chambers, 9/1 M G Road, *Tel 584144*
Chung Wah Restaurant, Residency Road, *Tel 582662*
Koshy's Jewel Box (Mx), 39 St Mark's Road, *Tel 213793*
Khyber, 17/1 Residency Road, *Tel 212205*
Lotus, Ashok Hotel, Kumara Krupa, High Grounds, *Tel 269482/269462*
Mandarin (Ch), Ashok Hotel, Kumara Krupa, High Grounds, *Tel 269482/269482*
Memories of China (Ch), Taj Residency, 14 M G Road, *Tel 584444*
Princess (Mx), Curzon Complex, Brigade Road, *Tel 565679,* (Knock out Disco attached)
Southern Comfort (Coffee Shop SVg), Taj Residency, 14 M G Road, *Tel 568888,* (excellent appam and veg. stew)
The Rice Bowl, Hotel Rama, Lavelle Road, *Tel 572417*
The Peacock (Mx), 2 Residency Road, *Tel 213890*

Tiffany's (Mx), 23 Grant Road, *Tel 210377*
West End (Vg/NVg), Race Course Road, (poolside sit-out, good, grilled, Indian foods) *Tel 269281*
Windsor Manor (NVg), 25 Sankey Road, (typically English pub food, draught beer, fried fish and chips, shepherds pie) *Tel 268898*

MODERATE

Aishwarya (Ch, T), Gupta Market, K G Road, *Tel 200373*
Amaravathi (Vg, NVg), Off M G Road, *Tel 585140* (Andhra Food)
Bangalore International, High Grounds, *Tel 268011*
Berrys (Vg, NVg), Church Street, (North Indian non-veg dishes, particularly kadai type) *Tel 587383*
Chalukya (SVg), 44 Race Course Road, *Tel 265055*
Copacabana Bar & Restaurant, 18/1 Cambridge Road, *Tel 563694*
Canopy (Mx), Public Utility Bldg., *Tel 588542* (open-air roof top, good ambience)
Casa Piccola (Cont), Devatha, 131 Residency Road, *Tel 212907* (specialists in pizzas and profit rolls)
Chandrika (NVg), 9/1 Cunningham Road, *Tel 260197* (very good paneer masala and mushroom masala)
Chaupal Restaurant (NVg), Harsha Hotel, 11 Venkataswamy Naidu Road, *Tel 565566*
Dolphin, 131/2 Wheeler Road, Cox Town, *Tel 573073*
Four Seasons, 20 R M Roy Road, *Tel 237453*
Kadai Restaurant (Vg/NVg), 130/1 Wheeler Road, Cox Town, (For good N. Indian, especially non-veg dishes)
Konark (Vg), 98 Residency Road, *Tel 214799*
Koshy's (Mx), 39 St Mark's Road, *Tel 213793* (good Cont. food)
Mac's Fast Food (pizzas, burgers, all sorts of icecreams and pastries) *Tel 586205*
Mobo's Restaurant (Mx), 72 III Cross, Mission Road, *Tel 223067*
Nagarjuna Residency (Vg, NVg), 44/1 Residency Road (Andhra food) *Tel 585130*
Nanking (Ch), 3 Grant Road, *Tel 214301*
Oasis, 186/1 S C Road, S D Puram *Tel 361437*
Pavillion, Ist Main, S D Puram, *Tel 367683*
Rice Bowl (Ch), 215 Brigade Road, *Tel 587417*
RR Brigades (Vg, NVg), Church Street, *Tel 586060* (Andhra food)
Rumali (NVg), Church Street (excellent rumali rotis and black dal)
Sapna (NVg), 69/40 Residency Road, *Tel 584689* (south Indian snacks and fresh fruit juices)
Shangri La (Ch), 182 Brigade Road, *Tel 588994* (good Tibetan momos and hot and sour soup)
Silver Plate (Ch), 2 Residency Road
Sip In (Vg, NVg), 4 Mavalli Tank Bund Road, *Tel 223689,* (Andhra and North Indian food)
Sona (M, Ch), 236/1 Subedar Chatram Road, (Near Anand Rao Circle)
Step Inn (Vg, NVg), 43/4 8th Main, Malleswaram, *Tel 367164,* (good Punjabi and Chinese fare)

Tandoor, 28 M G Road, *Tel 584620*
The Only Place (Cont), 161 Brigade Road, *Tel 572440,* (excellent steaks and apple pie)
Ullas Refreshments (Vg), Public Utility Bldg., M G Road, *Tel 584711* (snacks mainly, good rasam vadai, excellent coffee)

INEXPENSIVE

Cellar Snack Bar, 11 Brigade Road, *Tel 563471*
India Coffee House, Brigade Road, *Tel 372860* (specialises in manglorean food, excellent cold coffee)
Kamat Restaurant (SVg), Unity Bldgs., J C Road, *Tel 224802*
Mavalli Tiffin Rooms (Vg), 2-C Lalbagh Road, *Tel 220022* (the place in town for s. Indian snacks)
Nilgiris Restaurant (NVg), Brigade Road, (sandwiches, patties, snacks)
Parag (SVg, NVg), open air restaurant (south Indian snacks, north Indian food and draught beer.
Seven Star Sagar, Talkies Bldg, *Tel 27064*
Shakti, Sampige Road, (delicious vegetarian meals)
Shyamaprakash (Vg), near Indian Express Bldg., (lovely garden restaurant, offers full meals for lunch. s and n. Indian snacks)
Sukh Sagar Food Complex, Majestic Square, *Tel 79189*
Taj Mahal, Old Poorhouse Road, Shivajinagar, (excellent kababs)
Veena Stores, 15th Cross, Margosa Road, Malleswaram (unbelievably good idlies, evenings only, and no sitting space)
Woodlands Restaurant (SVg), K E B complex, Kempe Gowda Road

TRAVEL AGENTS

Agents who retail package holidays and travel tickets can be found all over Bangalore

Bharat Travels (Karnataka), 3/2 St Marks Rd., *Tel 212251*
Globe Express Travels, 106 Richmond Rd., *Tel 213172*
International Travel Service, West End Hotel, Race Course Rd. *Tel 263898*
Ram Mohan and Co, Chamber of Commerce Building, Kempe Gowda Rd., *Tel 266885*
Revel Tours and Travels, 1A Mahatma Gandhi Rd., *Tel 566379*
Sita World Travels, St Marks Road, *Tel 569382*
Trade Wings, 26/1 Lavelle Rd., *Tel 214595*
Travel Corporation of India, 9/1 Residency Rd., *Tel 212826/9*

WORSHIP

Buddhist Temple at Maha Bodhi Society, 14 Kalidasa Road, Gandhi Nagar, *Tel 260684*

CHRISTIAN

All Saints (Methodist), 1 Hosur Road, *Tel 572289*
Infant Jesus (Roman Catholic), Rose Garden, Vivek Nagar, *Tel 577206*
St Marks Cathedral (Protestant), Mahatma Gandhi Road, *Tel 213633*
St Mary's Basilica (Roman Catholic), Shivaji Nagar, *Tel 578274*

HINDU

Banashankari Temple, Banashankari
Bull Temple, Basavangudi
Gavi Gangadhareshwara Temple, Gavipuram
Someshwara Temple, Ulsoor
Subramanya Temple, Ulsoor

JAIN

Swetambara temple at Chickpet, Gandhinagar, Sajjan Rao Circle, and Jayanagar, *Tel 73678*
Digambara Temple at Chickpet

MUSLIM

Jumma Masjid, Old Poor House Street
Jami Masjid, City Market
Military Masjid, St John's Road

PARSI

Fire Temple Queen's Road, *Tel 564258*

SIKH

Gurudwara, Kensington Road (Nr Ulsoor Lake), *Tel 573461*

Directory of Services – Mysore

ACCOMMODATION

Luxury above Rs 1000
Moderate Rs 500 – 1000
Economy Rs 100 – 500

LUXURY

Dasaprakash Paradise, Yadavagiri, *Tel 25555/32368*
Krishnarajasagar, Brindavan Gardens, K R Sagar, Belagola, *Tel (Belagola) 22*
Lalit Mahal Palace, Siddharthanagar, *Tel 26316*
Metropole, 5 JLB Road, *Tel 31916/31967*
Southern Star, 13-14 Vinoba Road, *Tel 27217*

MODERATE

Brindavan, Bangalore Nilgiri Road, *Tel 24550*
Dasaprakash, Gandhi Square, *Tel 24455/24444*
Highway, Sayyaji Rao Road End, New Bannimantap Extn. *Tel 21534*
Kalinga, K R Circle, *Tel 31310*
King's Court, JLB Road, *Tel 25250*
Maurya Hoysala, JLB Road, *Tel 25349*
Ritz, Bangalore Nilgiri Road, *Tel 22668*
Siddhartha, 73/1 Guest House Road, Mazarbad, *Tel 26869*

ECONOMY

Aashraya, Dhanvantri Road, *Tel 27088*
Anand Vihar Lodge, Makkaji Chowk, *Tel 20809*
Anugraha, Sayyaji Rao Road, *Tel 20581*
Arun, 424 Jagan Mohan Palace, Desika Road, *Tel 30252*
Athithya, Dhanvantri Road, *Tel 25466*

Balaji Lodge, near Gandhi Square.
Chalukya, Rajkamal Talkies Road, *Tel 27197*
Chakravarthy, Ashoka Road, *Tel 32526*
Cauvery, Devaraj Urs Road, *Tel 27376*
Dashrath, Opposite Zoo, *Tel 2121*
Dyrkar, Gandhi Square.
Gokul, D Banumaiah Square, *Tel 27555*
Gupta, 252/B Ashoka Road, *Tel 33002/35089*
Indra Bhavan, Dhanvantri Road, *Tel 23933*
Karthik, Chandragupta Road, *Tel 31244*
Kaveri, 369 Chalunamba Agrahara, *Tel 26816/30351*
Lakshmi Lodge, Shivarampet, *Tel 22316*
Madhu Nivas, Gandhi Square, *Tel 23363*
Maharaja, JLB Road, *Tel 26665*
Maurya, Hanumantha Rao Road, *Tel 26677*
New Gayathri Bhavan Dhanvantri Road, *Tel 21224*
Palace Lodge, Opposite Jaganmohan Palace.
Panchami, behind Sangam Theatre, *Tel 34862*
Parimala, Krishnavilas Road, *Tel 27387*
Prakash, Sayyaji Rao Road, *Tel 22506*
Sagar Lodge, Dhanvantri Road Cross, *Tel 21029*
Sandesh, 3 Nazarbad Main Road, *Tel 35588/23210*
Sarmas, Jaganmohan Palace, Desika Road, *Tel 32243*
Sriram,Sayyaji Rao Road, *Tel 27111*

OTHERS

Railway Retiring Rooms

AIRLINES

Indian Airlines, 2 Jhansi Laxmibai Road, Hotel Mayura Hoysala complex, *Tel 21846*
Vayudoot, GSA Mysore International Travel Agency, 66/A Chamaraja Road, *Tel 22020*

BANKS

Andhra Bank, 105/106 Devaraj Urs Road, *Tel 25602*
Canara Bank, Statue Square, *Tel 21426*
Central Bank of India, 3/4 K R Circle, *Tel 23135*
Indian Bank, Gandhi Square, *Tel 23576*
Indian Overseas Bank, Old Bank Road, Gandhi Square, *Tel 23573*
Sate Bank of India, New Sayyaji Rao Road, *Tel 25274*
State Bank of Mysore, Ashoka Road, *Tel 25073*
Syndicate Bank, K R Circle, *Tel 23926*
Vijaya Bank, Near K R Circle, *Tel 23926*
Vysya Bank, Devaraj Urs Road, *Tel 221565*

CHEMISTS

(Open *0830 – 2200*)

City Drugs and Opticals, Sayyaji Rao Road, *Tel 23760*
Lakshmi Narayan Medical Stores, Dhanvantri Road, *Tel 21046*
Narasimha Medicals, Off Temple Road, V Mohalla
Prashanth Chemists and Druggists, Ashoka Circle, *Tel 32933*
Raghulal and Company, 207 Sayyaji Rao Road, *Tel 20733*

(Open 24 hours)
All night medical stores attached to K R Hospital and Mission Hospital

CINEMAS

Ganesh, Laxmipuram, *Tel 20432*
Gayatri, Double Road, *Tel 23568*
Laxmi, Chamaraja Double Road
Ledo, Ooty-Bangalore Road,
Prabha Picture House, Old Bank Road, *Tel 23569*
Sangam, Halkadakeri, *Tel 20044*
Shalimar, Tilaknagar, *Tel 23688*
Shantala, Narayana Sastry Road, *Tel 23299*
Stirling, Visveswara Nagar, *Tel 21170*

HOSPITALS

ALLOPATHIC

Aditya Hospital, I Main Contour Road, Gokulam III Stage, *Tel 37332/36332*
Ashoka Hospital, Krishnamurthypuram, *Tel 23945*
Basappa Memorial, Vinoba Road, J L Puram, *Tel 26401*
Epidemic Diseases Hospital, Bamboo Bazaar, *Tel 23801*
Gunamba Maternity and Child Welfare Trust and Indian Red Cross Society, V V Road, *Tel 23859*
Holsworth Memorial (Mission) Hospital, Sawday Road, *Tel 22715/21650*
Kamakshi Hospital, Kuvempunagar, *Tel 23945*
Ravi Nursing Home, Yadavagiri, *Tel 20746*
St Mary's Hospital, Chamundipuram, *Tel 22089*

INDIAN

College of Indian Medicine Hospital, Irwin Road, *Tel 26741*

RESTAURANTS

EXPENSIVE

Jewel Rock Restaurant (Mx), Off Statue Square, (the Ch Vg items are particularly good.)
King's Kourt (Mx), JLB Road, *Tel 25250* (try the hot and sour fish)
Lalith Mahal Palace Restaurant (Mx), Siddharta Nagar, *Tel 27650* (good dinner buffet and tandoori items.)
Metropole (Mx), JLB Road, *Tel 20681* (by far the best tandoori items in Mysore.)
Southern Star (Mx), Vinoba Road, *Tel 27217*

MODERATE

Copper Chimney (Mx), Kalidasa Road, (good soups)
Dasaprakash Paradise Vivekananda Road, Yadavagiri
Durbar (Mx), Old Bank Road, (tandoori items are good)
Paras (Mx), Sayyaji Rao Road, *Tel 20236*
Park Lane, (NVg), Sri Harsha Road, *Tel 30400*
Punjabi Restaurant (T), Dhanvantri Road
RR (NVg), Next to Sangam Talkies, (off Chandragupta Road)
Ritz (Mx), Bangalore – Nilgiri Road, *Tel 22668*
SR (S & NVg), Chalukya, Off Dhanvantri Road
(try the chicken pepper fry)
Samrat (NVg), Dhanvantri Road, *Tel 23933*
Shilpashri Restaurant and bar (M & T), Gandhi Square, *Tel 25979*
Tandoor Restaurant (T), Dhanvantri Road
Toot-C (Fast Food), Akashvani Circle, Yadavagiri, *Tel 25449* (try the chicken mayonnaise roll and mushroom pizza)
Top Stuff (Mx), Kalidasa Road, (very good butter chicken)

INEXPENSIVE

Athithya (SVg)
Bombay Tiffany's (NVg), Sayyaji Rao Road, *Tel 21087*
Central Lunch Home (S & NVg), Ashoka Road, *Tel 20760*
Dasaprakash (Svg), Gandhi Square, *Tel 24455* (good lunch thalis)
Gayatri Tiffin Room (SVg), Chamundipuram Circle
Golden Bowl Restaurant (Fast Food), Double Road, Kuvemp Nagar
Gopika (SVg)
Indra Bhavan (S & NVg), Dhanvantri Road, *Tel 23933*
Indra's Sweet 'n' Spice (Vg), Kalidasa Road, *Tel 36733*
Indra's (SVg, Fast Food, Vg & Snacks), Devaraj Urs Road
Kamadhenu (SVg), Sayyaji Rao Road, *Tel 21171*
Kamat Hotel & Sweets (SVg), Chandragupta Road, *Tel 26837*
Khatta Meetta (SVg), Dhanvantri Road, *Tel 27088*
Madhu Nivas (SVg), Gandhi Square, *Tel 23363*
Modern Cafe (SVg), Sayyaji Rao Road
Murali Cafe (SVg)
New Gayatri Bhavan (Vg), Dhanvantri Road, *Tel 21224*
Prasad Lunch Home (SVg)

Preetham Refreshments (Vg), Devraj Urs Road
Ramya (SVg), Dr Radhakrishna Marg, *Tel 26140* (tasty set dosai)
Raj Bhavan (SVg), J M Palace Square, *Tel 23110*
Saviruchi (SVg)
Vasu Nalpak (Svg), 131 Devraj Urs Road, *Tel 30733*
Vinayaka (SVg), Nazarabad, (good set dosai)

TRAVEL AGENTS

Bharat International Travels, 6-7 Municipal Hostel Building, Chamaraja Double Road, *Tel 24462*
Mysore International Travel Agency, 66/A Chamaraja Double Road, *Tel 22020*
Siddharta Tours and Travels, Hotel Siddharta, 73/1 Government Guest House Road, Nazarabad, *Tel 26869*
Travel Corporation of India, 35/A IV Main Road, Vidhyaranyapuram, *Tel 27100*

WORSHIP

Christian

St Bartholomews Church (Protestant), Church Street
St Philomena's Church (Catholic), Ashoka Road
Wesley Cathedral (Protestant), Bangalore–Ooty Road

HINDU

Chamundi Temple, Chamundi Hill
Eshwara Temple, Temple Road, V V Mohalla
Kote Anjaneya Temple, Palace North Gate
Lakshmi Venkataramanaswamy Temple, K R S Road, V V Mohalla
Mookambika Temple, Gokulam Park Road
Parakal Mutt, near Jagan Mohan Palace
Sri Ganesh Temple, Palace North Gate
Sri Raghavendra Mutt, near Shantala Theatre
Venkataramana Temple, Ventikoppal

MUSLIM

Masjid-e-Jafferey, 9th Cross, Akbar Road

REFERENCE

(For Sectional Maps)

Predominantly Built-up Area, Important Building ....

Predominantly Unbuilt Area ....

Predominantly Green Area ....

Water Body ....

Railways:

Broad Gauge ....

Metre Gauge ....

Railway Station and Bridge ....

Roads according to importance and Road Bridge:

On scale 1:16,500
(6 cm = 1 km) ....

On scale 1:25,000
(4 cm = 1 km) ....

Hospital, Dispensary, Clinic ....

Temple, Mosque, Church ....

Post Office, Telegraph Office .... *PO* *TO*

Post and Telegraph Office .... *PTO*

Police Station .... *PS*

Tourist Information Centre ....

Cinema, Auditorium ....

Hotel, Restaurant ....

Bus Terminal/Stand/Station ....

AROUND BANGALORE & MYSORE

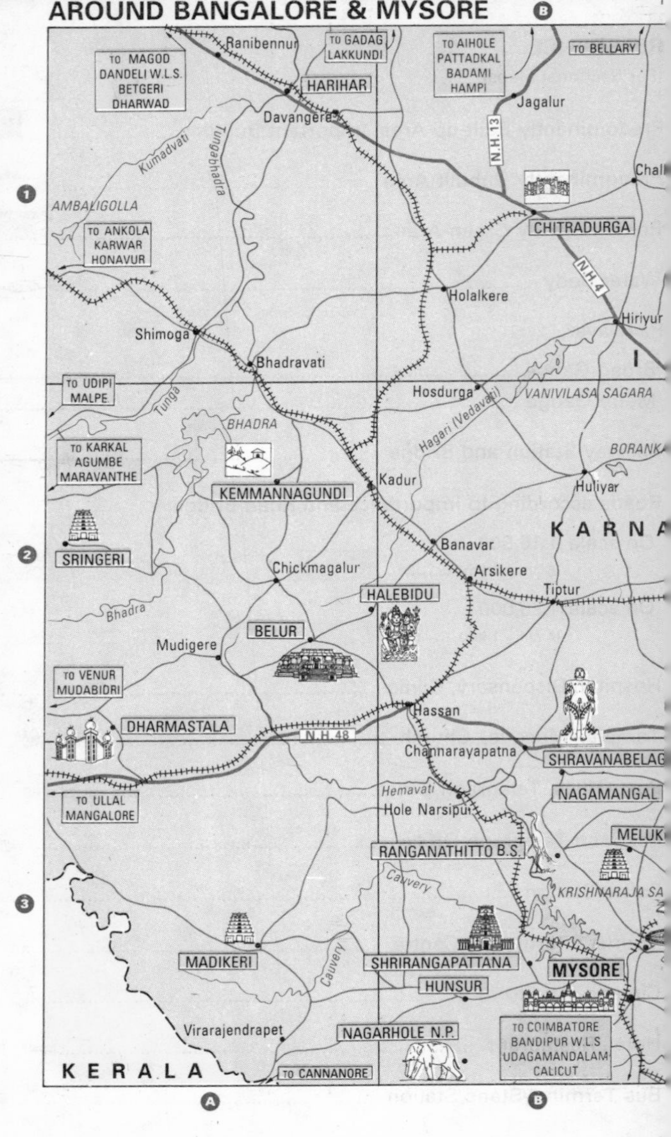

: 1:2,000,000 (1 cm = 20 km)

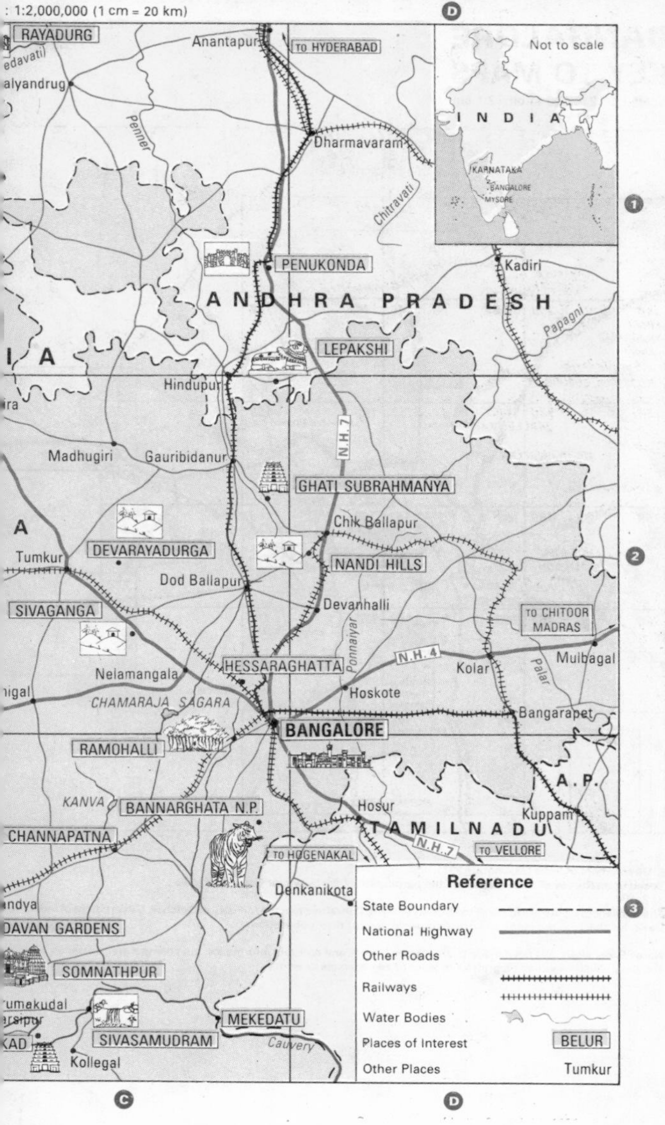

BANGALORE
KEY TO MAPS

Scale : 1 : 210,000 (1 cm=2.1 km)

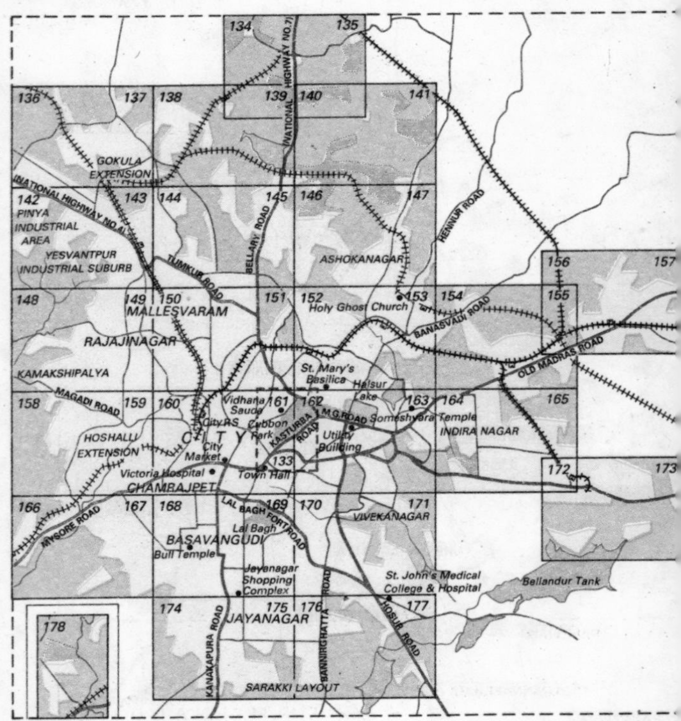

Based upon Survey of India maps with the permission of the Surveyor General of India .

The publishers would like to thank the Survey of India, Dehradun, and the Ministry of Defence, Government of India, New Delhi, for checking the maps and granting pemission for their publication.

Note : Every effort has been made to provide up-to-date and accurate information but changes are constantly occuring and the publishers would be grateful to learn of any changes or errors.

Scale : 1:16,500(6 cm=1 km)

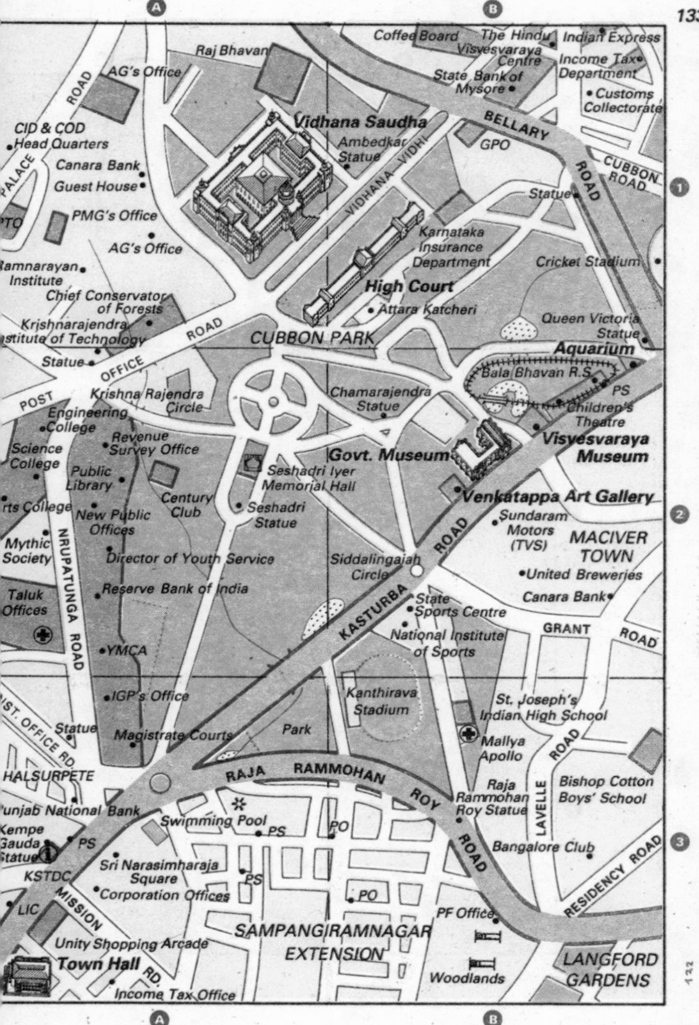

Based upon Survey of India map with the permission of the Surveyor General of India.

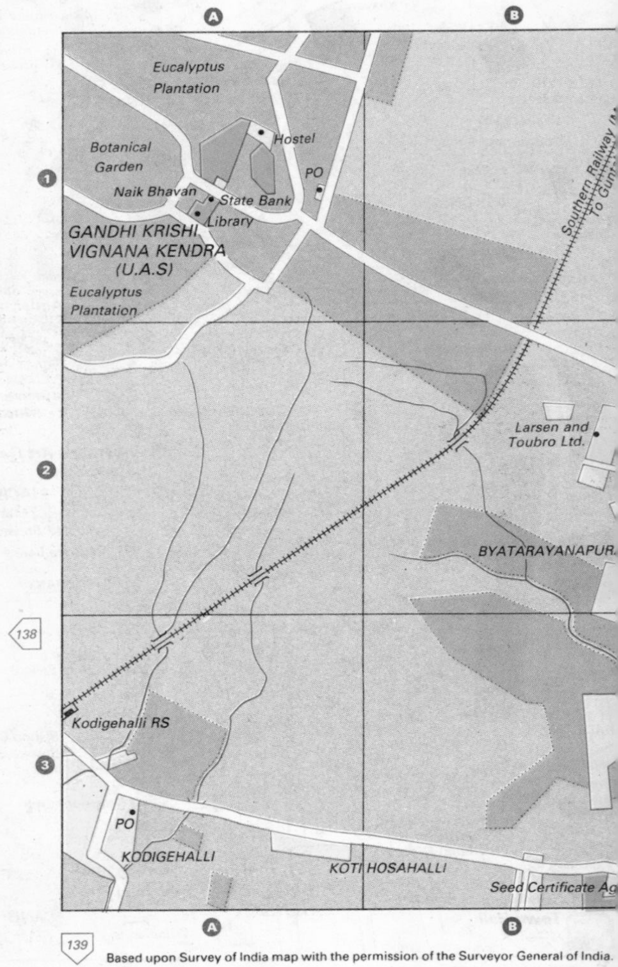

Based upon Survey of India map with the permission of the Surveyor General of India.

ale : 1:25,000 (4 cm = 1 km)

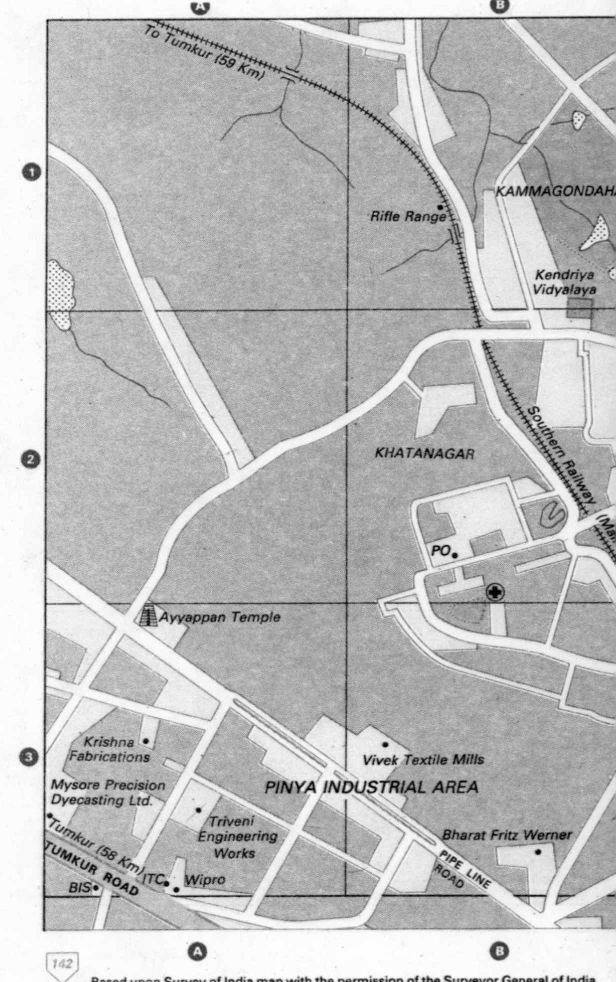

142

Based upon Survey of India map with the permission of the Surveyor General of India.

e : 1:25,000 (4 cm = 1 km)

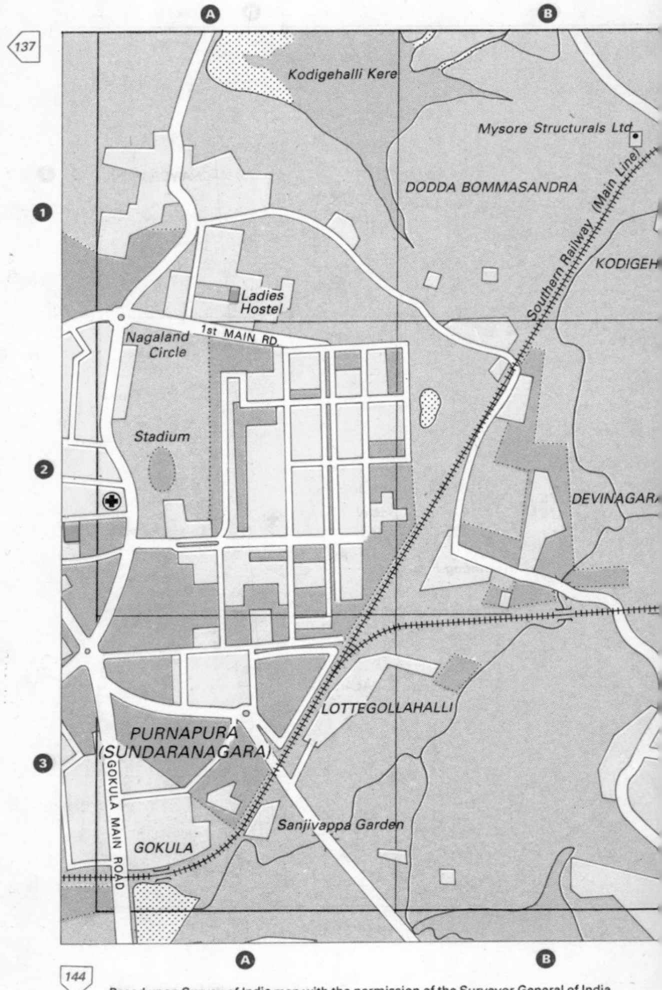

Based upon Survey of India map with the permission of the Surveyor General of India.

ale : 1:25,000 (4 cm = 1 km)

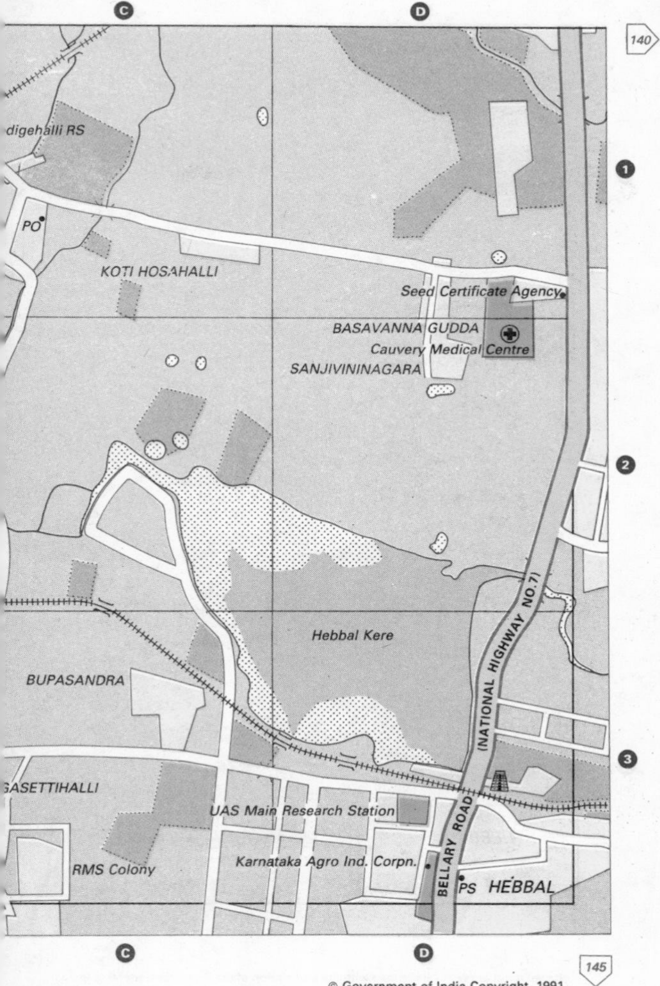
C
D
140
digehalli RS
1
PO
KOTI HOSAHALLI
Seed Certificate Agency
BASAVANNA GUDDA
Cauvery Medical Centre
SANJIVININAGARA
2
NATIONAL HIGHWAY NO.7
Hebbal Kere
BUPASANDRA
3
GASETTIHALLI
UAS Main Research Station
BELLARY ROAD
Karnataka Agro Ind. Corpn.
RMS Colony
PS
HEBBAL
C
D
145

135

139

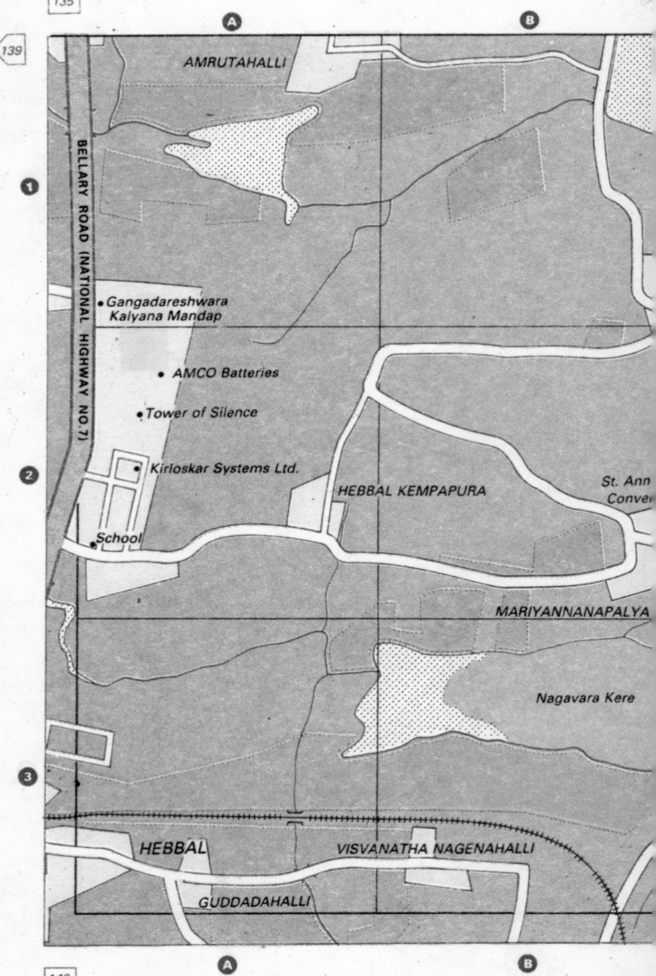

146

Based upon Survey of india map with the permission of the Surveyor General of India.

ale : 1:25,000 (4 cm = 1 km)

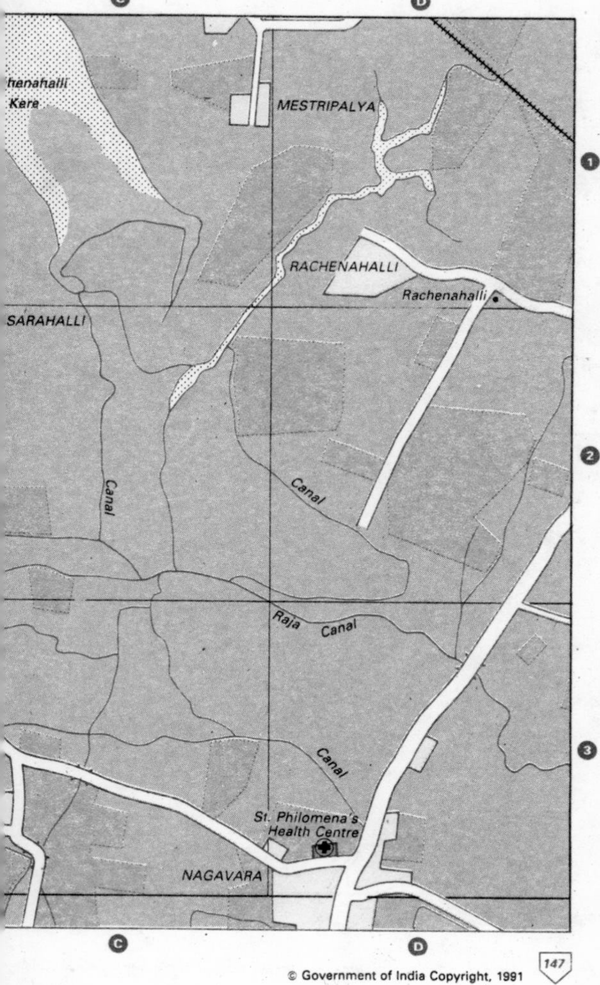

147

136

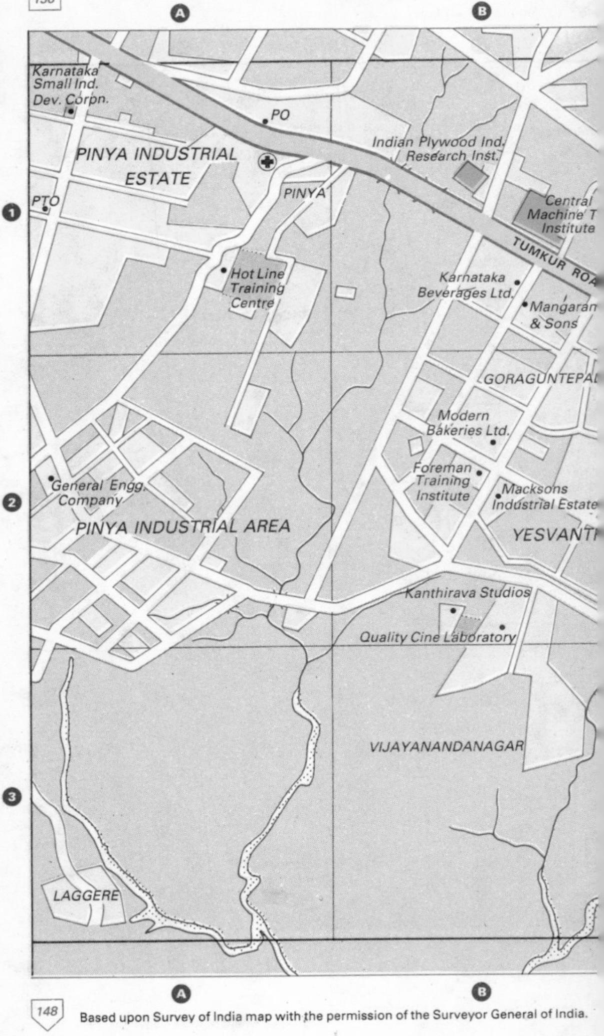

148

Based upon Survey of India map with the permission of the Surveyor General of India.

e : 1:25,000 (4 cm = 1 km)
C
D
137
144
TANNIRHALLI
Matti Kere
Tata Finlay Ltd
Tata Tea Ltd
PIPE LINE ROAD
Kurlon Factory
HMT LAYOUT
1
Fire Brick & Potteries Ltd.
ATIONAL HIGHWAY No 4
Mysore Electricals
Eskay Metals
IOL
Railway Quarters
Sri Maruti Textiles
2
PO
ISTRIAL SUBURB
GOUTAMAPURA
YESVANTPUR
Market
PTO
Weldcraft Testing Lab.
Indo German Plantation Machinery Co.
Mysore Electro-Chemical Works Ltd
Intercon Engineers
Hindustan Cement Products
Swissind Fitters
3
Govt. Soap Factory
ASHOKAPURAM
Foundry (Kirloskar Electric Co. Ltd)
Rajendra Spinning Mills
CHORD ROAD
80 FEET ROAD
PO
PO
Swimming Pool
Mysore Fruit Products
RAJAJI NAGAR
MAHALAKSHMI LAYOUT
INDUSTRIAL SUBURB
C
D
149

138

143

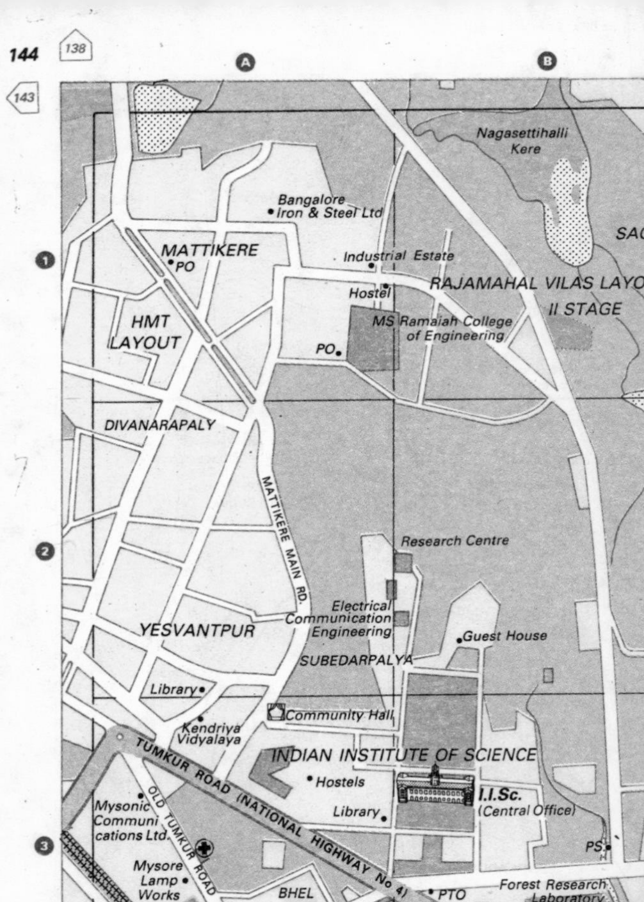

150

Based upon Survey of India map with the permission of the Surveyor General of India.

le : 1:25,000 (4 cm = 1 km)

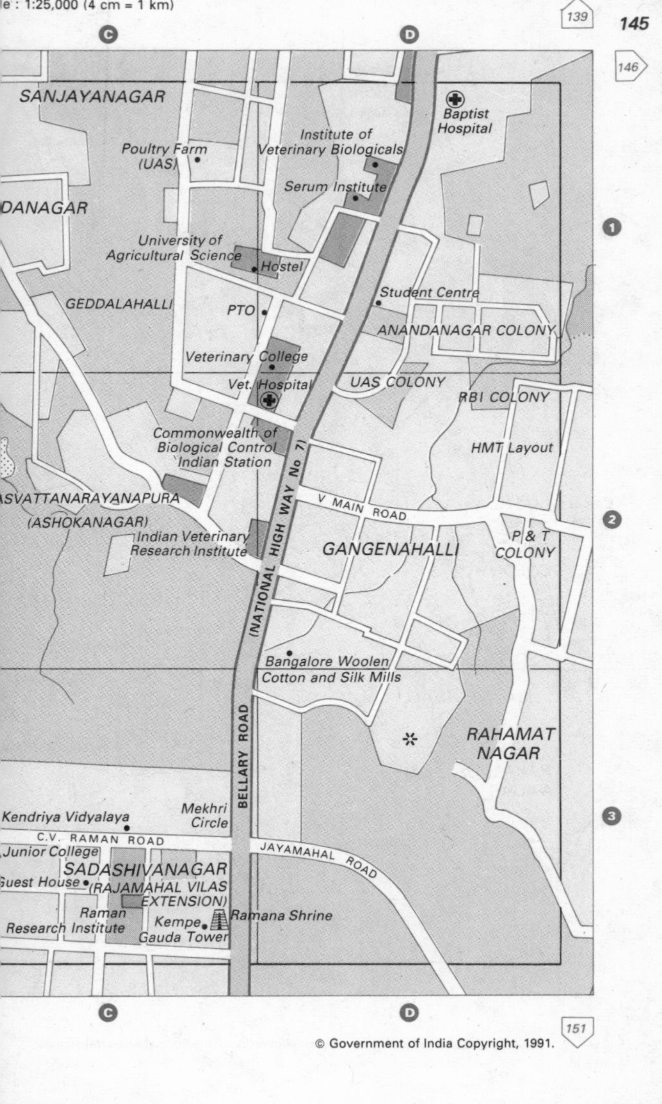

Based upon Survey of India map with the permission of the Surveyor General of india.

▮e : 1:25,000 (4 cm = 1 km)

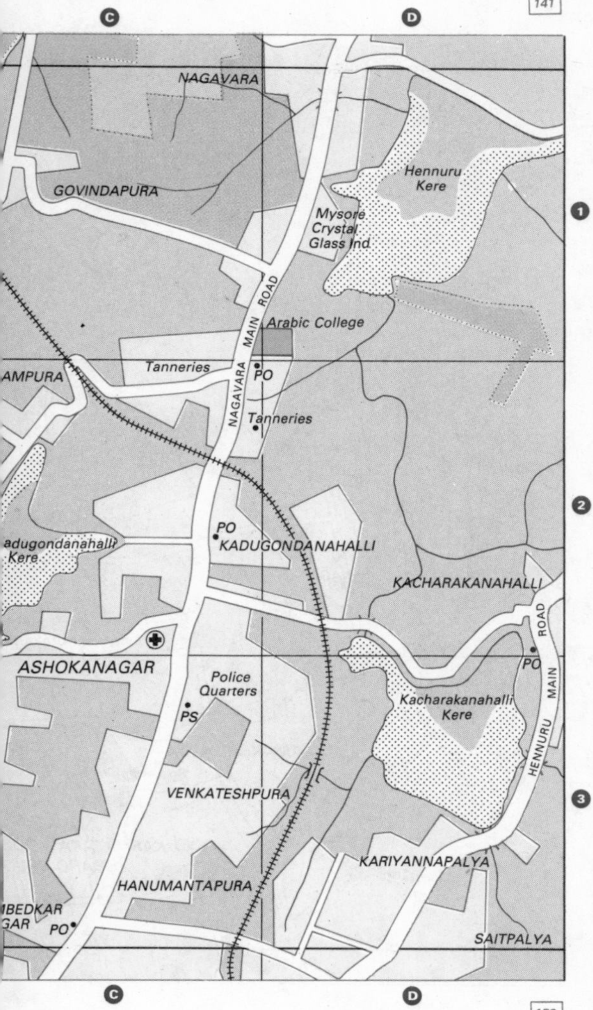
141
C
D
NAGAVARA
Hennuru
Kere
GOVINDAPURA
Mysore
Crystal
Glass Ind
1
NAGAVARA MAIN ROAD
Arabic College
AMPURA
Tanneries
PO
Tanneries
2
PO
KADUGONDANAHALLI
adugondanahalli
Kere
KACHARAKANAHALLI
ASHOKANAGAR
HENNURU MAIN ROAD
PO
Police
Quarters
PS
Kacharakanahalli
Kere
VENKATESHPURA
3
KARIYANNAPALYA
HANUMANTAPURA
BEDKAR
GAR
PO
SAITPALYA
C
D
153

142

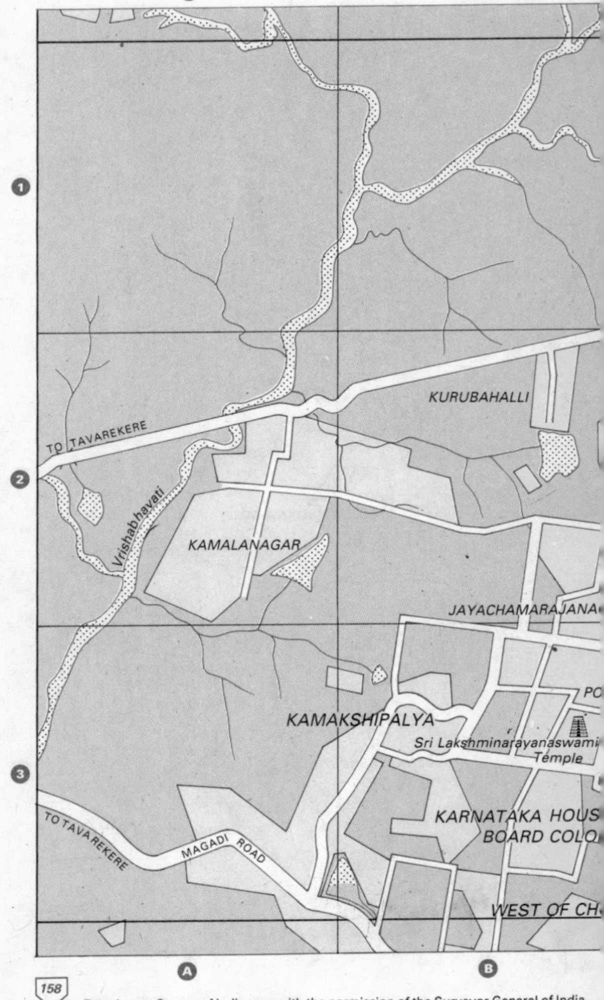

158

Based upon Survey of India map with the permission of the Surveyor General of India.

e : 1:25,000 (4 cm = 1 km)

C
D
143
150
Sri Prasanna
Viranjaneya Temple
Guest Keen
Williams Ltd.
Kirloskar
Electric Co.
College
MILK
COLONY
XVII CROSS
ROAD
WEST OF CHORD ROAD II STAGE
(NAGAPURA)
RAMNAGAR
SUBRAMANYA
NAGAR
Gudda
Hospital
80 FEET ROAD
1
CHORD ROAD
Sub Registrar's
Office
PTO
PO
G.D. Naidu
Institute
RAJAJINAGAR
I BLOCK
RAJAJINAGAR
II STAGE
PS
PS
nkar
Math
KETAMARNAHALLI
I CROSS ROAD
Eye Hospital
NCERT
BURIAL GROUND ROAD
WEST OF
CHORD ROAD III STAGE
2
INDIRANAGAR
RAJAJINAGAR
Nijalingappa
College
PS
80 FEET ROAD
Library
KEB Office
RAJAJINAGAR
II BLOCK
SIVANAHALLI
SANEGURUVANAHALLI
ESI Hospital
BOVI COLONY
Central Store
RAJAJINAGAR III BLOCK
ST OF CHORD ROAD I STAGE
3
Ramamandir
RA COLONY
D IV STAGE
RAJAJINAGAR
INDUSTRIAL TOWN
BHASHYAMNAGAR
Polytechnic
C
D
159

144
149
A
B
1
2
3
Kirloskar Electric Co.
PTO
Range Forest Office
Kendriya Vidyalaya
Arbindo Bhavan
IDL Chemical
XVII CROSS ROAD
VII MAIN ROAD
GAYATRI PARK EXTESION
RANGANATHAPU
Teachers Training Ins
Sri Chitrapur Math
Ladies Club
SUBRAMANYA NAGAR
XV CROSS ROAD
MARGOSA ROAD
VENKATARANGEINGAR ROAD
Cluny Convent
Homeopathic College and Hospital
MALLESVARAM
PO
KODANDA
RAJAJINAGAR II STAGE
GAYATRINAGAR
Hot Line Training Centre
Indian Statistical Institute
PO
MARUTI EXTESTION
MARI APPANAPALYA
VIII CROSS ROAD
Gandhi Bhavan
GUTTAH
PO
BURIAL GROUND ROAD
RAMAMOHANAPURAM
RAJAJINAGAR
V CROSS ROAD
PS
KC General Hospital
NAGAPPA BLOCK
ERRAPPA BLOCK
PTO
PRAKASHNAGAR
LAKSHMINARAYANAPURAM
PO
Mysore Spinning & Manufacturing Mills
Park Corporatio North Zon Office
SESH
SRI RAMPURAM
80 FEET ROAD
BHASHYAMNAGAR
HANUMANTAPURA
PLATFORM ROAD
Central Excise
SAIBABANAGAR
PO
RAMACHANDRAPURA
PTO
CGHS Dispensary
Industrial Estate
160

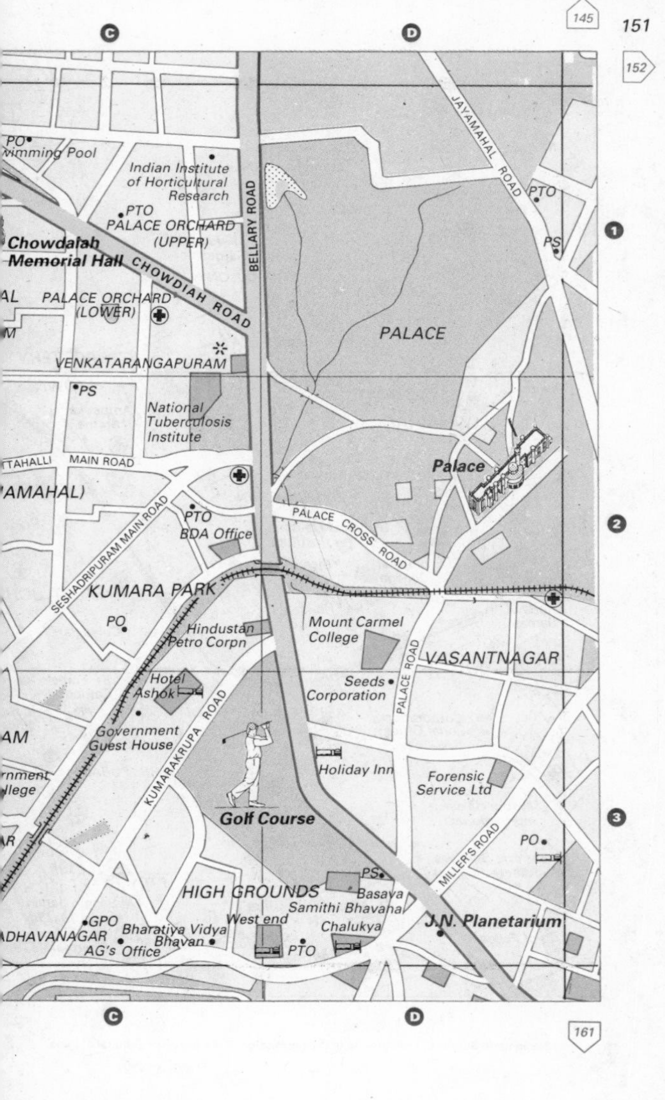

145
152
161
C
D
1
2
3
PO
Swimming Pool
Indian Institute
of Horticultural
Research
PTO
PALACE ORCHARD
(UPPER)
Chowdaiah
Memorial Hall
CHOWDIAH ROAD
BELLARY ROAD
JAYAMAHAL ROAD
PTO
PS
PALACE ORCHARD
(LOWER)
PALACE
VENKATARANGAPURAM
PS
National
Tuberculosis
Institute
MAIN ROAD
(JAYAMAHAL)
Palace
PTO
BDA Office
SESHADRIPURAM MAIN ROAD
PALACE CROSS ROAD
KUMARA PARK
PO
Hindustan
Petro Corpn
Mount Carmel
College
VASANTNAGAR
PALACE ROAD
Hotel
Ashok
Seeds
Corporation
Government
Guest House
KUMARAKRUPA ROAD
Holiday Inn
Forensic
Service Ltd
Golf Course
PO
MILLER'S ROAD
PS
HIGH GROUNDS
Basava
Samithi Bhavana
J.N. Planetarium
GPO
West end
Chalukya
Bharatiya Vidya
Bhavan
MADHAVANAGAR
AG's Office
PTO

146
151

A B

1 2 3

Health Unit
MUNIREDDIPALYA
Annaiyappa Block
CHURCH ROAD
Muddamma Garden
ITI COLONY
CHINNAPPA GARDEN
NANDIDURG ROAD
RAMASVAMIPALYA
POTTERY TOWN
Dr. Ambedkar Statue
JAYAMAHAL
JAYAMAHAL ROAD
NANDIDURG ROAD EXTENSION
BENSON TOWN
CLEVELA
COLES
HAINES ROAD
Hostel
Technical Training Institute
Theological College
Bishop's House
MILLER'S ROAD
ST. JOHN
Kodava Samaja
Rail House
Coles Park
MILLER'S ROAD
RS
St. Francis Xavie Cathedral
PO
Corporation Zonal Office
CSI Hospital
BROADWAY ROAD
SEPPINGS ROAD
NARAYANA PILLAI STREET
NEHRUPURAM
Tuberculosis Dispensary
Mysore Sales International
QUEEN'S ROAD
SHIVAJINAGAR
BHAR NAG
Banking Services (Southern Region)
PTO
TCH Tra
St. Mary's Basilica
Sangin Jamin Masjid
Commissioner of Police
CHANDNI CHOWK RD.
Russel Market
Dharmaraja Tem
Gosha

A B

162

Based upon Survey of India map with the permission of the Surveyor General of India.

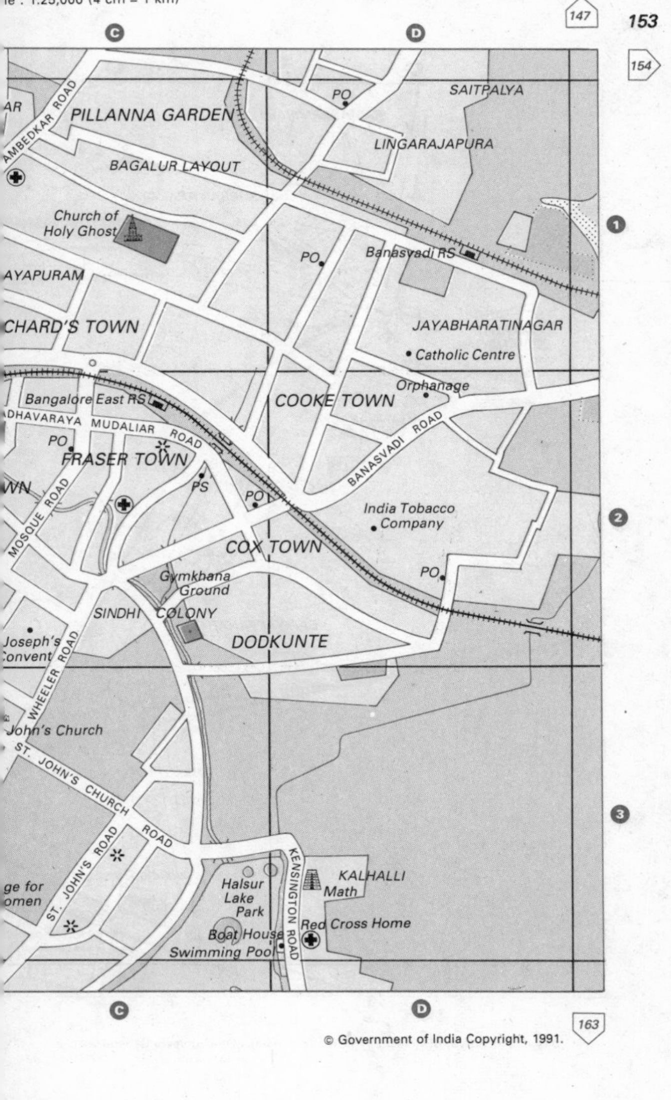
C
D
AR
AMBEDKAR ROAD
PILLANNA GARDEN
PO
SAITPALYA
LINGARAJAPURA
BAGALUR LAYOUT
Church of
Holy Ghost
PO
Banasvadi RS
AYAPURAM
CHARD'S TOWN
JAYABHARATINAGAR
Catholic Centre
Orphanage
Bangalore East RS
COOKE TOWN
DHAVARAYA MUDALIAR ROAD
PO
FRASER TOWN
BANASVADI ROAD
WN
MOSQUE ROAD
PS
PO
India Tobacco
Company
COX TOWN
PO
Gymkhana
Ground
SINDHI COLONY
Joseph's
Convent
DODKUNTE
WHEELER ROAD
John's Church
ST. JOHN'S CHURCH ROAD
ST. JOHN'S ROAD
KENSINGTON ROAD
KALHALLI
Math
Halsur
Lake
Park
ge for
omen
Red Cross Home
Boat House
Swimming Pool
C
D
1
2
3

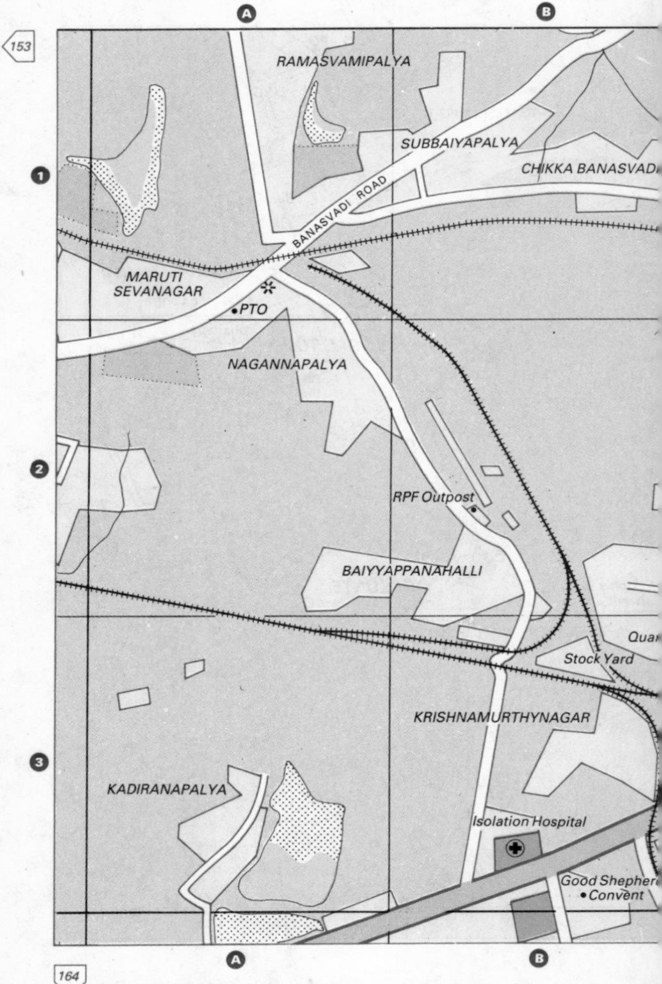

Based upon Survey of India map with the permission of the Surveyor General of India.

e : 1:25,000 (4 cm = 1 km)

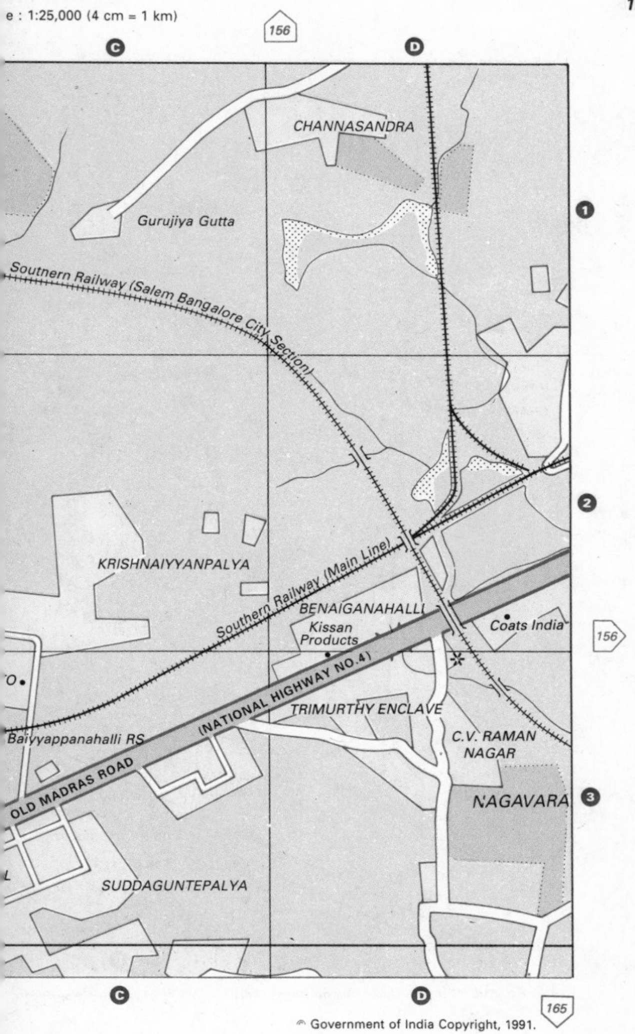

156

C

D

CHANNASANDRA

Gurujiya Gutta

Soutnern Railway (Salem Bangalore City Section)

1

2

KRISHNAIYYANPALYA

Southern Railway (Main Line)

BENAIGANAHALLI

Kissan Products

Coats India

156

O•

(NATIONAL HIGHWAY NO.4)

TRIMURTHY ENCLAVE

Baiyyappanahalli RS

OLD MADRAS ROAD

C.V. RAMAN NAGAR

NAGAVARA

3

L

SUDDAGUNTEPALYA

C

D

165

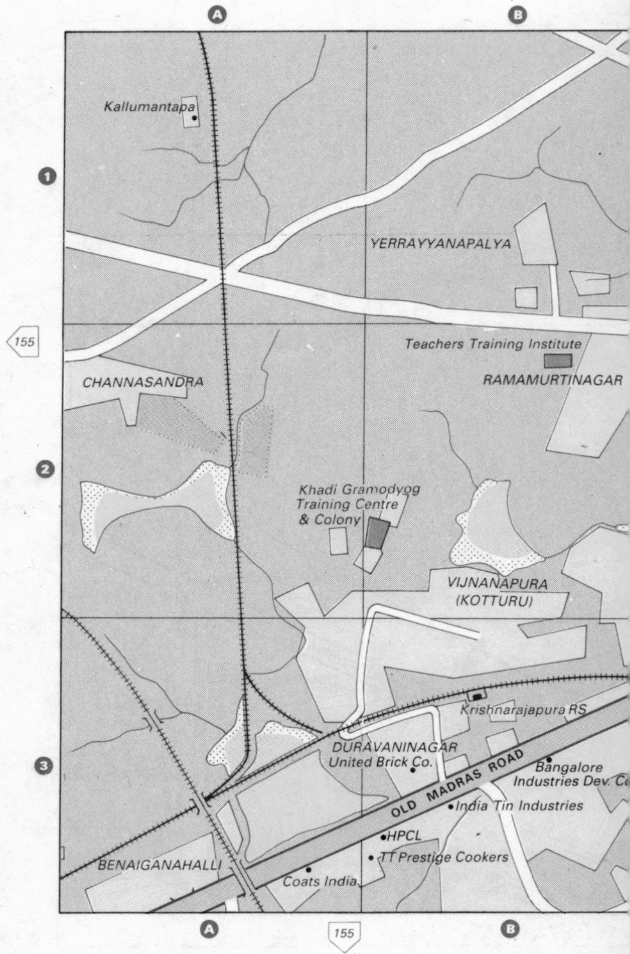

Based upon Survey of India map with the permission of the Surveyor General of India.

le : 1:25,000 (4 cm = 1 km)

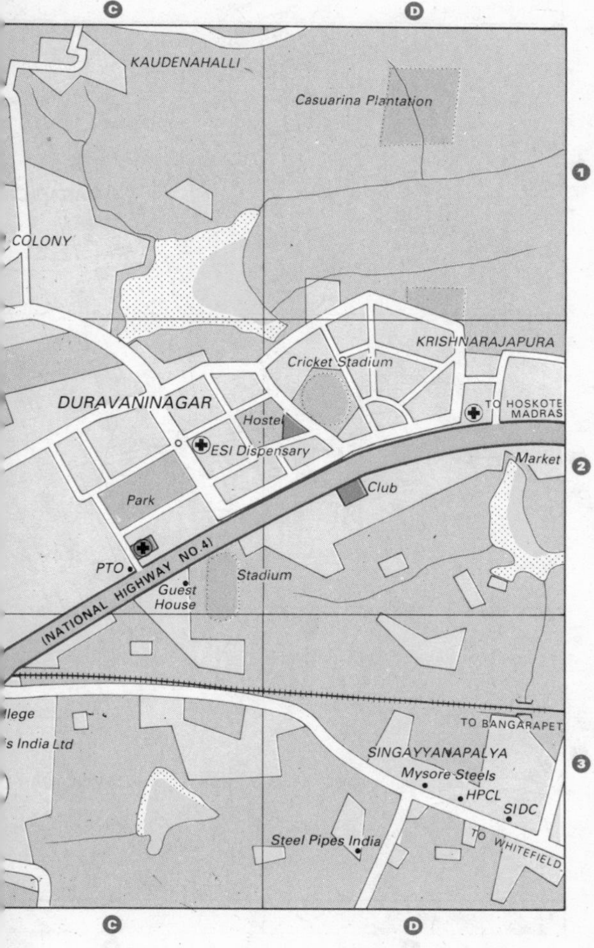
C
D
KAUDENAHALLI
Casuarina Plantation
1
COLONY
KRISHNARAJAPURA
Cricket Stadium
DURAVANINAGAR
Hostel
TO HOSKOTE
MADRAS
ESI Dispensary
Market
2
Club
Park
PTO
(NATIONAL HIGHWAY NO.4)
Stadium
Guest
House
llege
's India Ltd
TO BANGARAPET
SINGAYYANAPALYA
3
Mysore Steels
HPCL
SIDC
TO WHITEFIELD
Steel Pipes India
C
D

148

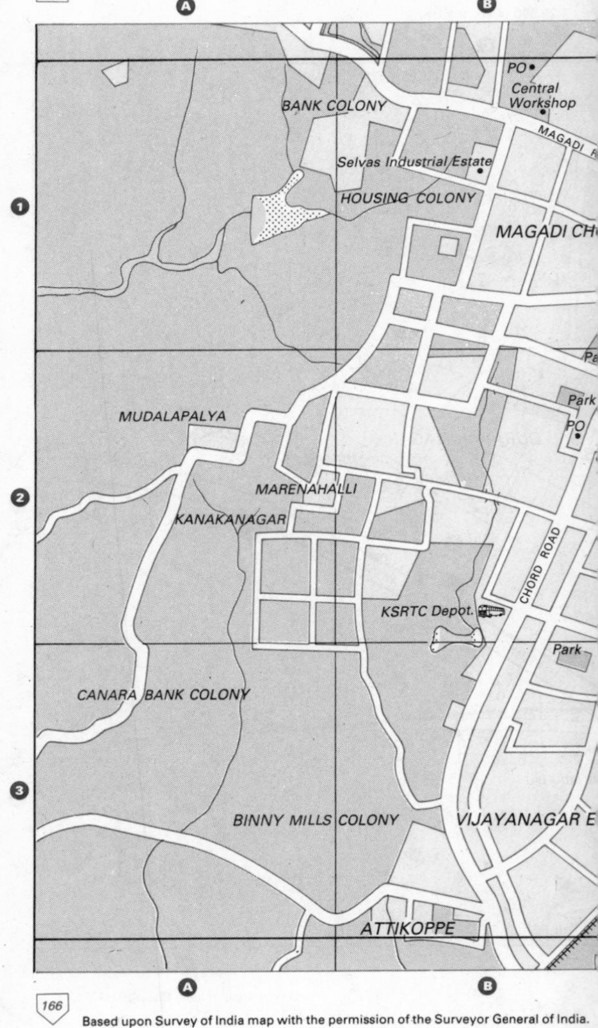

166

Based upon Survey of India map with the permission of the Surveyor General of India.

e : 1:25,000 (4 cm = 1 km)

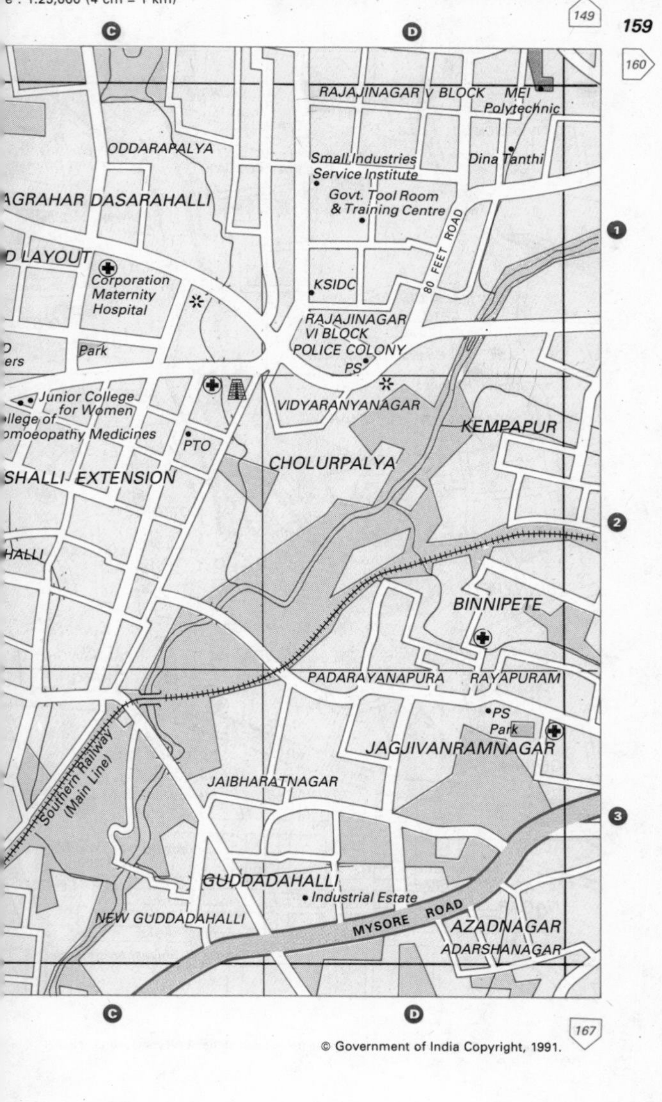
C
D
149
160
RAJAJINAGAR V BLOCK
MEI Polytechnic
ODDARAPALYA
Small Industries Service Institute
Dina Tanthi
AGRAHAR DASARAHALLI
Govt. Tool Room & Training Centre
80 FEET ROAD
1
D LAYOUT
Corporation Maternity Hospital
KSIDC
RAJAJINAGAR VI BLOCK
POLICE COLONY
PS
Park
Junior College for Women
llege of
omoeopathy Medicines
VIDYARANYANAGAR
KEMPAPUR
PTO
CHOLURPALYA
SHALLI EXTENSION
2
HALLI
BINNIPETE
PADARAYANAPURA
RAYAPURAM
PS
Park
JAGJIVANRAMNAGAR
Southern Railway (Main Line)
JAIBHARATNAGAR
3
GUDDADAHALLI
Industrial Estate
NEW GUDDADAHALLI
MYSORE ROAD
AZADNAGAR
ADARSHANAGAR
C
D
167

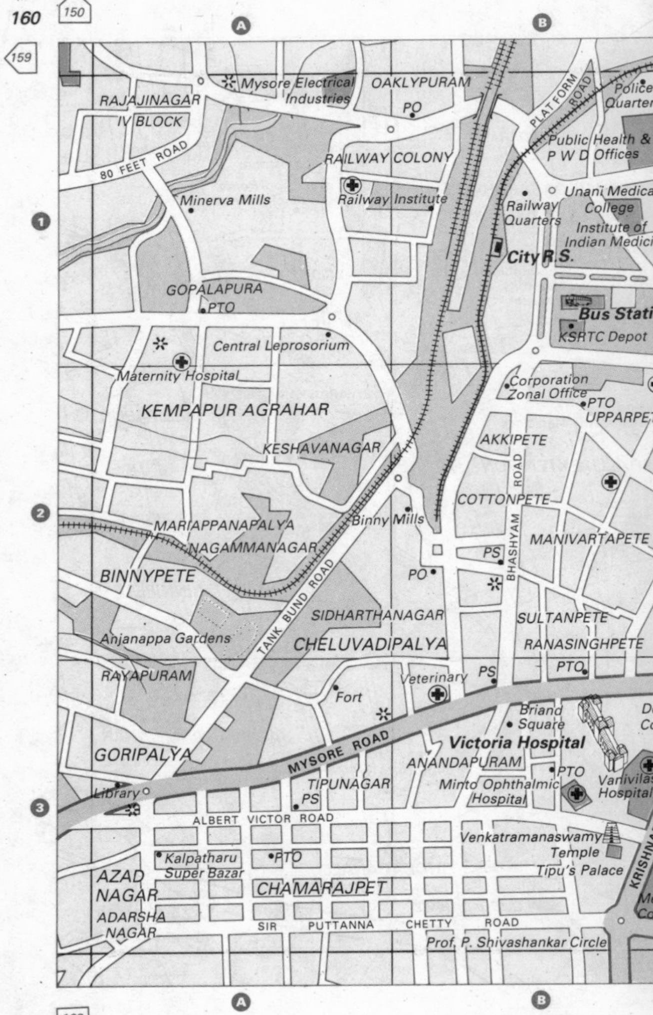

150
159
168
A
B
1
2
3
Mysore Electrical Industries
OAKLYPURAM
PO
RAJAJINAGAR IV BLOCK
80 FEET ROAD
PLAT FORM ROAD
Police Quarters
Public Health & P W D Offices
RAILWAY COLONY
Railway Institute
Minerva Mills
Unani Medical College
Railway Quarters
Institute of Indian Medicine
City R.S.
GOPALAPURA
PTO
Bus Station
KSRTC Depot
Central Leprosorium
Maternity Hospital
Corporation Zonal Office
PTO
UPPARPET
KEMPAPUR AGRAHAR
AKKIPETE
KESHAVANAGAR
ROAD
COTTONPETE
MARIAPPANAPALYA
Binny Mills
MANIVARTAPETE
NAGAMMANAGAR
PS
BHASHYAM
BINNYPETE
PO
TANK BUND ROAD
SIDHARTHANAGAR
SULTANPETE
Anjanappa Gardens
CHELUVADIPALYA
RANASINGHPETE
RAYAPURAM
Veterinary
PS
PTO
Fort
Briand Square
Victoria Hospital
GORIPALYA
MYSORE ROAD
ANANDAPURAM
PTO
TIPUNAGAR
Minto Ophthalmic Hospital
Vanivilas Hospital
Library
PS
ALBERT VICTOR ROAD
Venkatramanaswamy Temple
Kalpatharu Super Bazar
PTO
Tipu's Palace
AZAD NAGAR
CHAMARAJPET
ADARSHA NAGAR
SIR PUTTANNA CHETTY ROAD
Prof. P. Shivashankar Circle
KRISHNA

Based upon Survey of India map with the permission of the Surveyor General of India.

le : 1:25,000 (4 cm = 1 km)
C
D
151
162
1
2
3
SEE PAGE 133
Stable
Race Course
d Rao
SESHADRI ROAD
GANDHINAGAR
Commerce College
AG's Office
Legislators Home
Raj Bhavan
Vidhana Saudha
Guest House
PMG's Office
PTO
Ramnarayan Institute
VIDHANA VIDHI
Maharani's College
ROAD
Central Jail
PALACE
Central Observatory
Institute of Technology
High Court
Janata Bazar
PO
TO
Play Ground
Central College
K.R. Circle
KEMPE GAUDA ROAD
POST OFFICE ROAD
Arts College
Govt. Engineering College
Century Club
Seshadri Iyer Memorial Hall
Law College
Science College
Public Library
New Public Offices
District Court
NRUPATUNGA ROAD
CUBBON PARK
ate Bank of Mysore
PTO
Mythic Society
Siddalingaiah Circle
Junior College
Cauvery Bhavan
Reserve Bank of India
National Institute of Sports
URIUPETE
DISTRICT OFFICE ROAD
Taluk Offices
YMCA
I T Y
AVENUE ROAD
CUBBONPETE
KASTURBA RD.
Kanthirava Stadium
Ranganatha Temple
PO
IGP's Office
Park
PS
Magistrate Courts
TE ROAD
BALLAPURPETE
RAJA RAMMOHAN ROY ROAD
PETE
GANIGARPETE
NAGARTAPETE ROAD
Swimming Pool
DODPETE
PO
HALSURPETE
PS
PO
TO
NAGARTAPETE
KSTDC
Corporation Office
et
Jame Masjid
Khadi Gramodyog
Unity Shopping Arcade
SAMPANGI RAMNAGAR EXTENSION
Town Hall
MISSION RD.
Silver Jubilee Park
SRI NARASIMHARAJA ROAD
PTO
Ravindra Kalakshetra
College of Pharmacy
JAYACHAMARAJA WODEYAR ROAD
KALASIPALYA MAIN ROAD
TO
KUMBARAGUNDI
RAJA RAMMOHAN ROY EXTESTION
LAL BAGH ROAD
KENGAL HANUMANTAIAH ROAD
PTO
Transport Bhavan (KSRTC)
KALASIPALYA
169

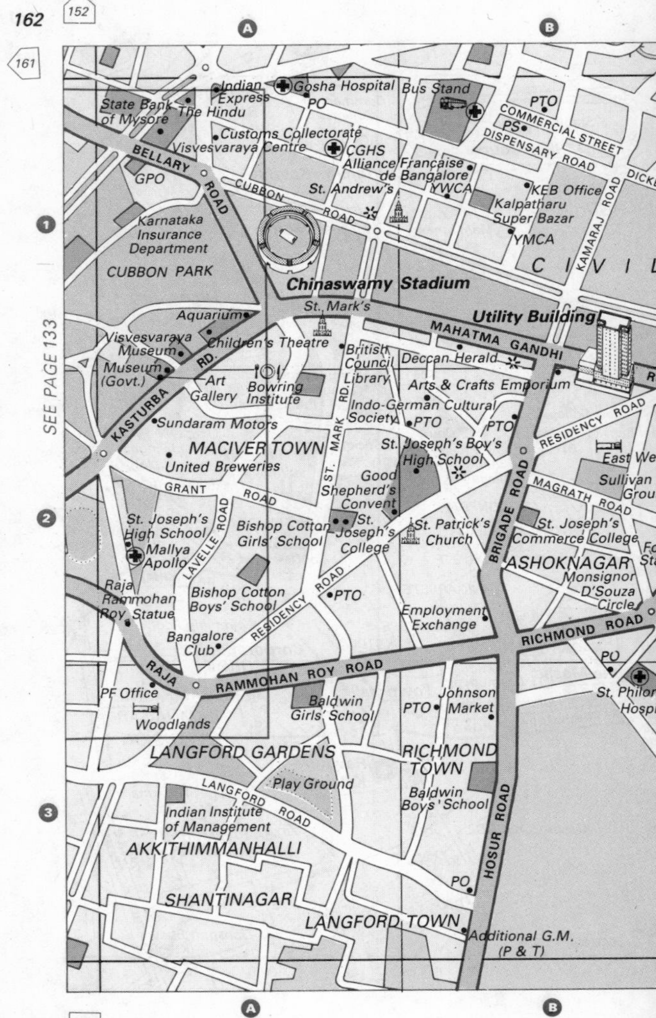
152
161
170
SEE PAGE 133
A
B
1
2
3
Indian Express
Gosha Hospital
Bus Stand
PO
PTO
State Bank of Mysore
The Hindu
COMMERCIAL STREET
PS
Customs Collectorate
DISPENSARY ROAD
Visvesvaraya Centre
CGHS
BELLARY ROAD
Alliance Française de Bangalore
GPO
CUBBON ROAD
St. Andrew's
YWCA
KEB Office
Kalpatharu Super Bazar
Karnataka Insurance Department
YMCA
KAMARAJ ROAD
CUBBON PARK
Chinaswamy Stadium
St. Mark's
Aquarium
Utility Building
Visvesvaraya Museum
Children's Theatre
MAHATMA GANDHI
British Council Library
Deccan Herald
Museum (Govt.)
Art Gallery
Bowring Institute
Arts & Crafts Emporium
KASTURBA RD.
Indo-German Cultural Society
Sundaram Motors
PTO
RESIDENCY ROAD
ST. MARK RD.
MACIVER TOWN
St. Joseph's Boy's High School
United Breweries
Good Shepherd's Convent
BRIGADE ROAD
GRANT ROAD
MAGRATH ROAD
Sullivan
St. Joseph's High School
LAVELLE ROAD
Bishop Cotton Girls' School
St. Joseph's College
St. Patrick's Church
St. Joseph's Commerce College
Mallya Apollo
ASHOKNAGAR
Monsignor D'Souza Circle
Raja Rammohan Roy Statue
Bishop Cotton Boys' School
RESIDENCY ROAD
Employment Exchange
Bangalore Club
RICHMOND ROAD
RAJA RAMMOHAN ROY ROAD
Johnson Market
PF Office
Baldwin Girls' School
Woodlands
LANGFORD GARDENS
RICHMOND TOWN
Play Ground
LANGFORD ROAD
Baldwin Boys' School
Indian Institute of Management
HOSUR ROAD
AKKITHIMMANHALLI
PO
SHANTINAGAR
LANGFORD TOWN
Additional G.M. (P & T)

Based upon Survey of India map with the permission of the Surveyor General of India.

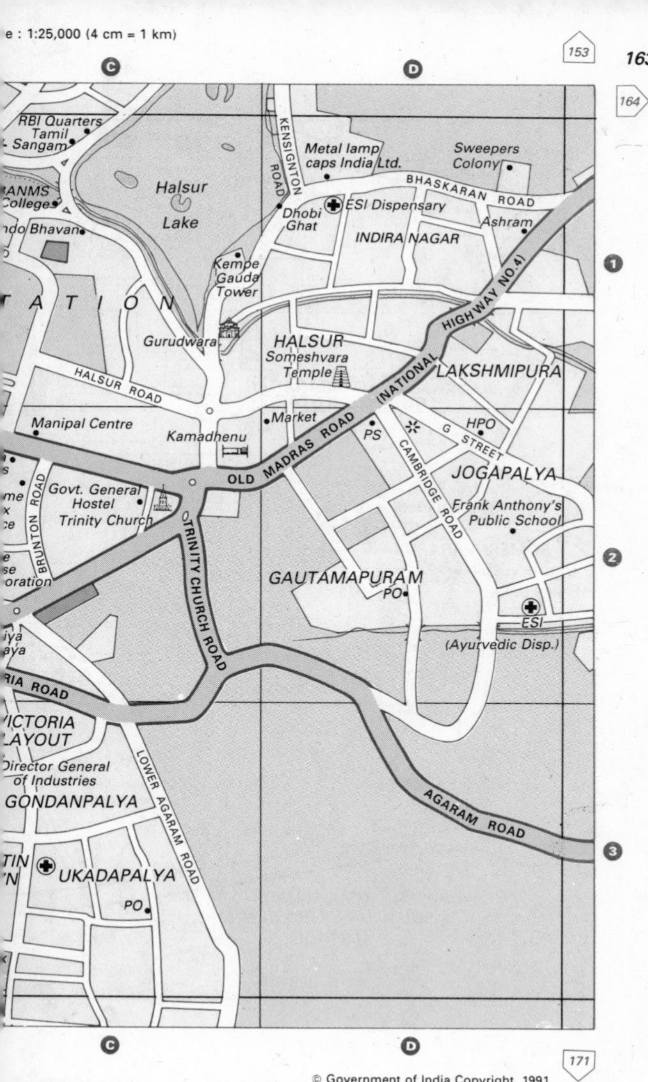
C
D
RBI Quarters
Tamil
Sangam
ANMS
College
ndo Bhavan
Halsur
Lake
KENSIGNTON
ROAD
Metal lamp
caps India Ltd.
Sweepers
Colony
BHASKARAN ROAD
ESI Dispensary
Dhobi
Ghat
Ashram
INDIRA NAGAR
Kempe
Gauda
Tower
TATION
HIGHWAY NO.4)
Gurudwara
HALSUR
Someshvara
Temple
(NATIONAL
LAKSHMIPURA
HALSUR ROAD
Market
PS
G STREET
HPO
Manipal Centre
Kamadhenu
OLD MADRAS ROAD
CAMBRIDGE ROAD
JOGAPALYA
BRUNTON ROAD
Govt. General
Hostel
Trinity Church
TRINITY CHURCH ROAD
Frank Anthony's
Public School
1
2
3
GAUTAMAPURAM
PO
ESI
(Ayurvedic Disp.)
RIA ROAD
VICTORIA
LAYOUT
Director General
of Industries
GONDANPALYA
LOWER AGARAM ROAD
AGARAM ROAD
UKADAPALYA
PO

154

163

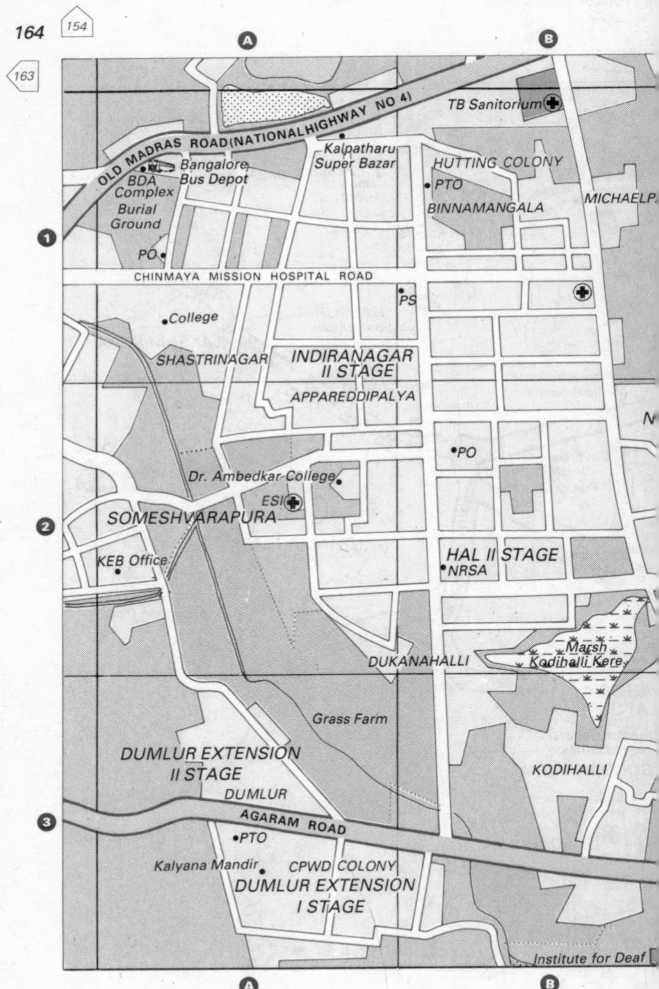
A
B
1
2
3
OLD MADRAS ROAD (NATIONAL HIGHWAY NO 4)
TB Sanitorium
Kalpatharu
Super Bazar
HUTTING COLONY
Bangalore
Bus Depot
BDA
Complex
PTO
Burial
Ground
BINNAMANGALA
MICHAELP
PO
CHINMAYA MISSION HOSPITAL ROAD
PS
College
SHASTRINAGAR
INDIRANAGAR
II STAGE
APPAREDDIPALYA
PO
Dr. Ambedkar College
ESI
SOMESHVARAPURA
KEB Office
HAL II STAGE
NRSA
DUKANAHALLI
Marsh
Kodihalli Kere
Grass Farm
DUMLUR EXTENSION
II STAGE
DUMLUR
KODIHALLI
AGARAM ROAD
PTO
Kalyana Mandir
CPWD COLONY
DUMLUR EXTENSION
I STAGE
Institute for Deaf

155
C
D
BAIRASANDRA
Bharat
Earth Movers
Southern Railway
1
HAL III STAGE
PPASANDRA
SURANJANDASS
ROAD
GARKAMANTAPALYA
URGAMPALYA
2
NALLUR GUDISALU
X MAIN ROAD
PS
JIVAN BIMANAGAR
172
NANJAREDDI COLONY
REDDIPALYA
ANANDANAGAR
3
hire Home India
Market
VIMANANAGAR
PS
PTO
ipal Hospital
Varma
Industries
MVPU College
RAMANAGAR
TO WHITEFIELD
C
D
172

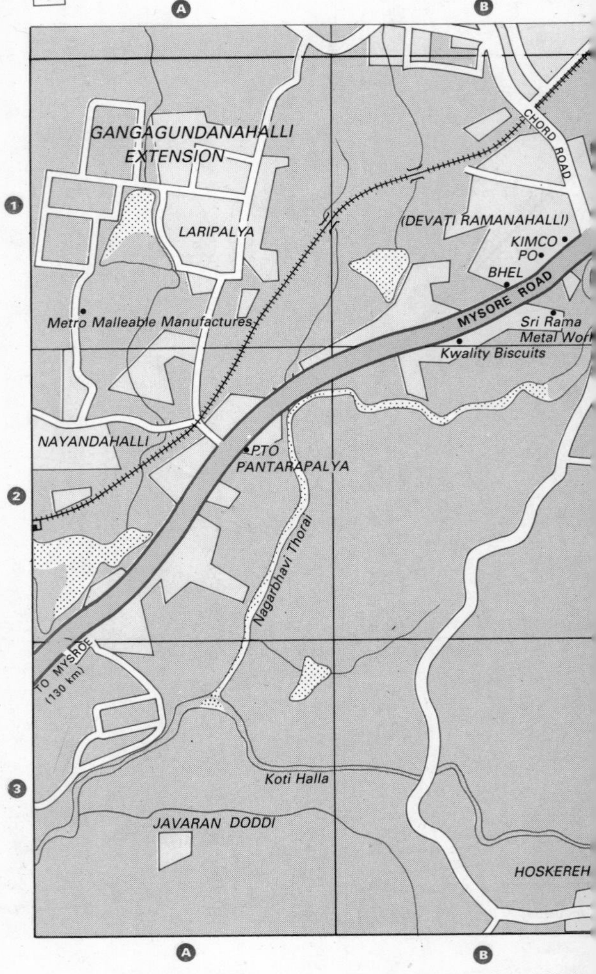

Based upon Survey of India map with the permission of the Surveyor General of India.

159

168

C
D
UJINAGAR
KARITHIMMANAHALLI
PO
PTO
MADIGARPALYA
AMCO
Batteries Ltd
Mysore Chrome
Tanning Co.
TIMBERYARD
LAYOUT
KATESHPURNAGAR
Mysore Machinery
Manufacturing
Kempe Gauda Tower
Dhobi
Ghat
BYATRAYANAPURA
SRINAGAR
DASARHALLI
AVALHALLI
NAGENDRA BLOCK
Junior College
BANK COLONY
GIRINAGAR
(WRITERS' COLONY)
Maternity Disp.
BANK COLONY
SRINIVASANAGAR
BANASHANKARI
LAYOUT III STAGE
1
2
3
C
D

160
167

174

Based upon Survey of India map with the permission of the Surveyor General of India.

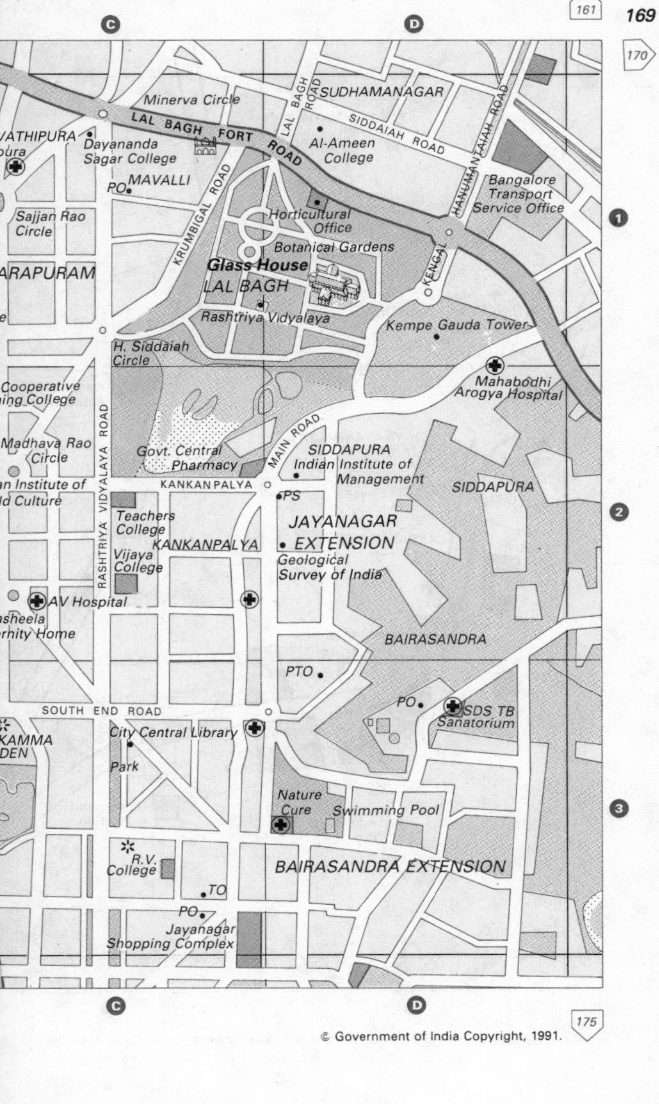
C
D
Minerva Circle
LAL BAGH FORT ROAD
SUDHAMANAGAR
LAL BAGH ROAD
SIDDAIAH ROAD
VATHIPURA
pura
Dayananda Sagar College
Al-Ameen College
HANUMANTAIAH ROAD
MAVALLI
PO
KRUMBIGAL ROAD
Bangalore Transport Service Office
Sajjan Rao Circle
Horticultural Office
Botanical Gardens
Glass House
LAL BAGH
KENGAL
ARAPURAM
Rashtriya Vidyalaya
Kempe Gauda Tower
H. Siddaiah Circle
Mahabodhi Arogya Hospital
Cooperative
ing College
MAIN ROAD
Madhava Rao Circle
Govt. Central Pharmacy
SIDDAPURA
Indian Institute of Management
SIDDAPURA
an Institute of
ld Culture
KANKANPALYA
PS
RASHTRIYA VIDYALAYA ROAD
Teachers College
JAYANAGAR EXTENSION
KANKANPALYA
Vijaya College
Geological Survey of India
AV Hospital
asheela
rnity Home
BAIRASANDRA
PTO
SOUTH END ROAD
PO
SDS TB Sanatorium
KAMMA
DEN
City Central Library
Park
Nature Cure
Swimming Pool
R.V. College
BAIRASANDRA EXTENSION
TO
PO
Jayanagar Shopping Complex
1
2
3

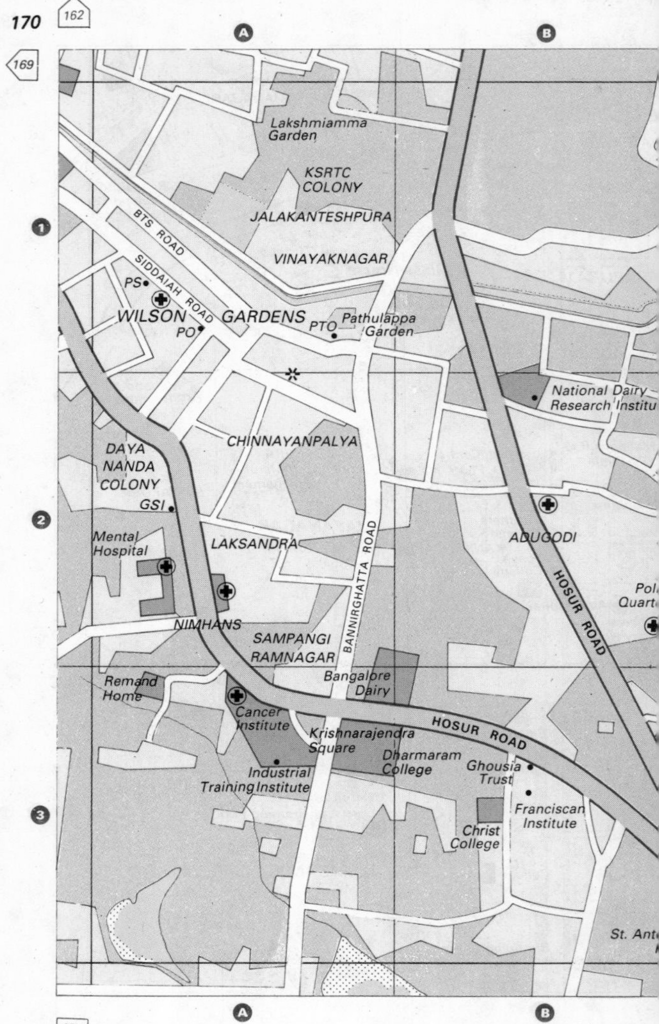

Based upon Survey of India map with the permission of the Surveyor General of India.

163
C
D
AUSTIN TOWN
EW TOWNSHIP
VANNARPET
PTO
Library
PS
SONENAHALLI
SANDRA
IJIPURA ROAD
VIVEKANAGAR
1
RAJENDRANAGAR
IJIPURA
Jayendra
TCH Training
School
2
KORAMANGALA
AYACHAMARAJANAGAR
rade Ground
Asst.
mmissioner of Police
KORAMANGALA LAYOUT
PO
KATTALPALYA
Chinnagara
Kere
PS
3
DUSTRIAL
AREA
Jyothi Nivas
College
MESTRIPALYA
JOHNNAGAR
St. John's Medical
College & Hospital
JAKASANDRA
BLOCK
C
D
177

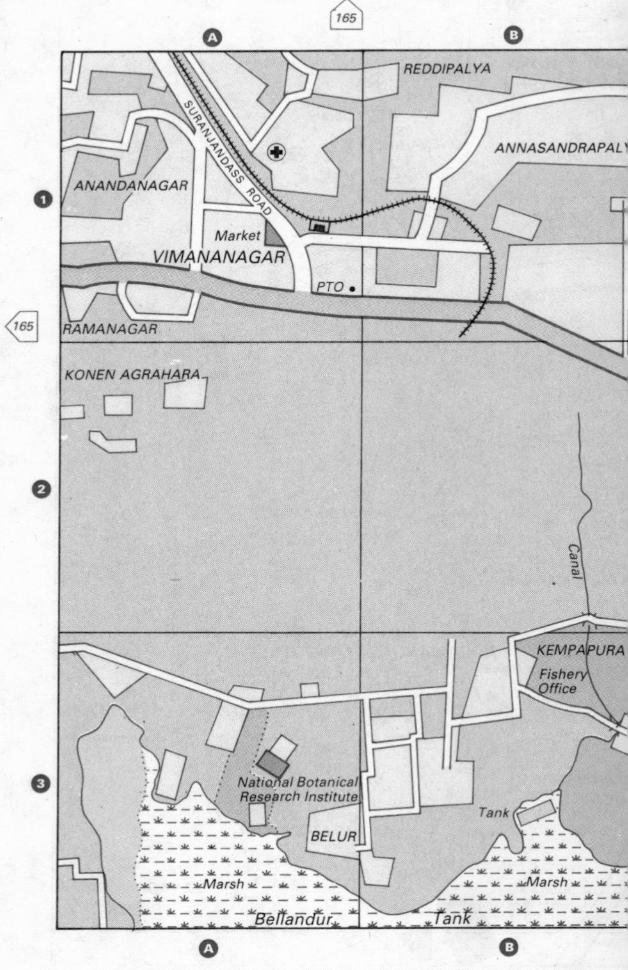

Based upon Survey of India map with the permission of the Surveyor General of India.

le : 1:25,000 (4 cm = 1 km)

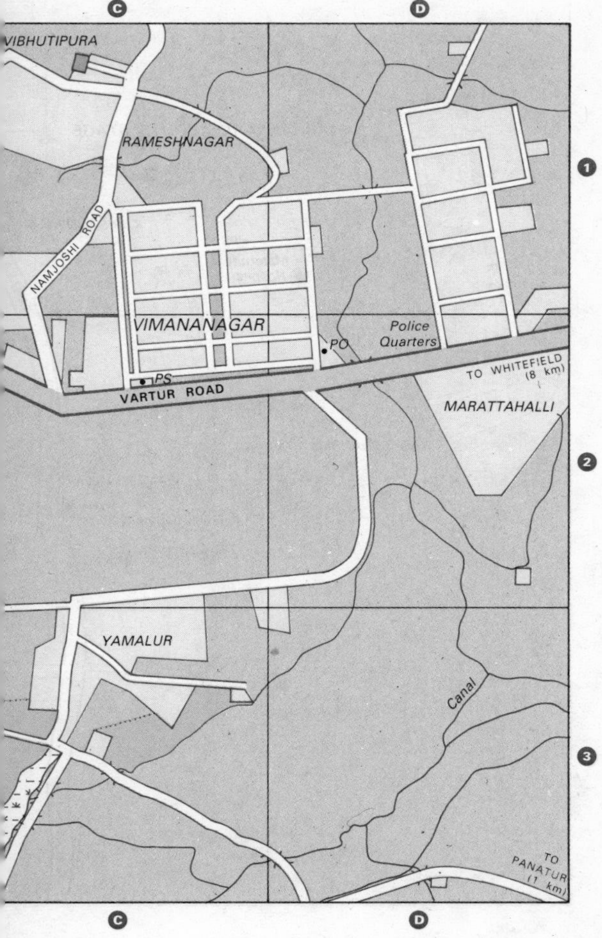

168

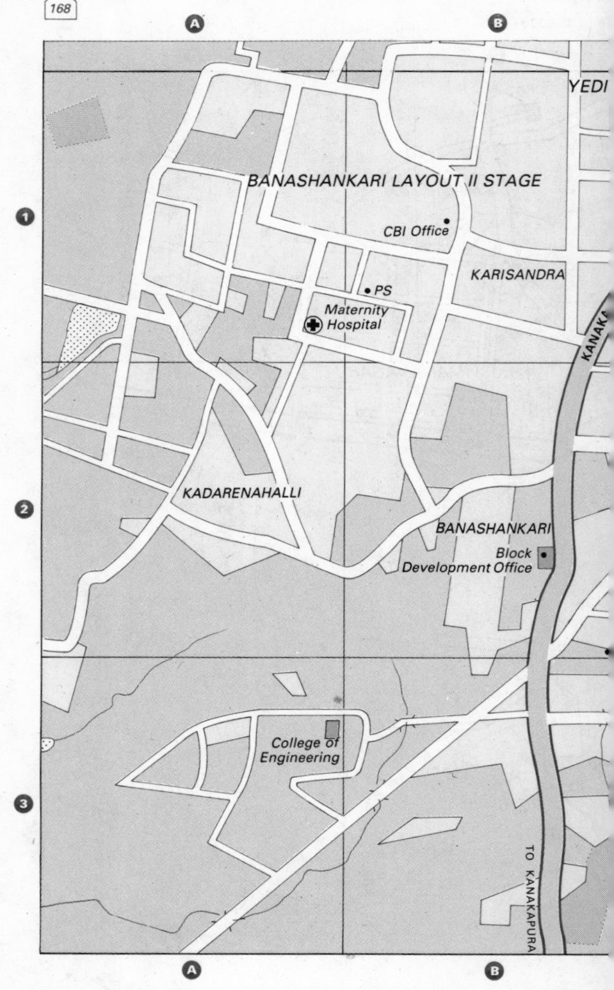

Based upon Survey of India map with the permission of the Surveyor General of India.

e : 1:25,000 (4 cm = 1 km)

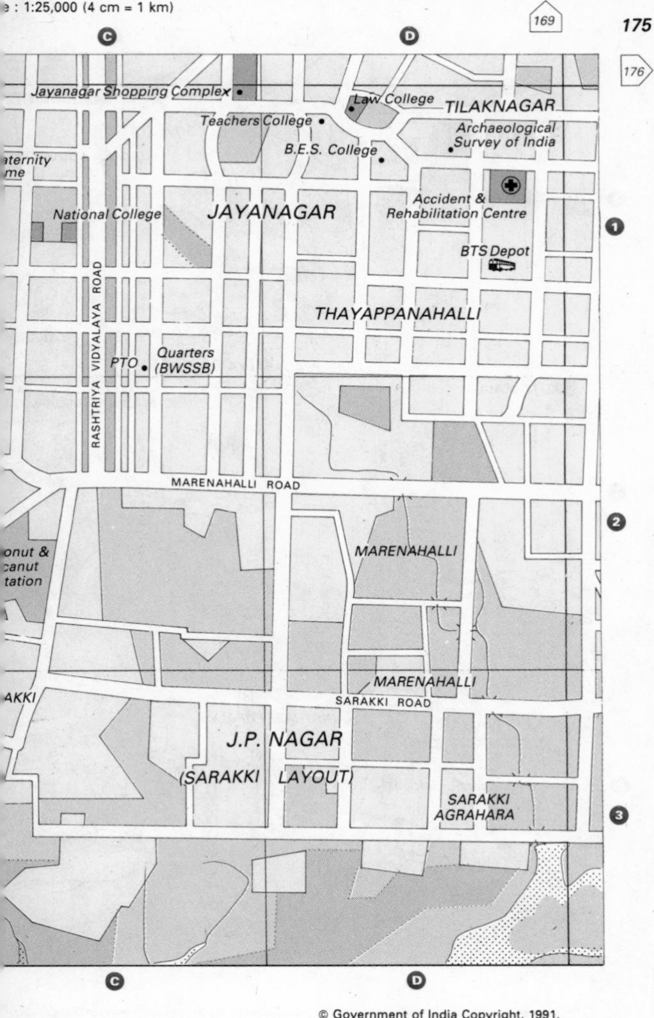

169
176
C
D
Jayanagar Shopping Complex
Law College
TILAKNAGAR
Teachers College
Archaeological Survey of India
B.E.S. College
aternity
me
Accident & Rehabilitation Centre
National College
JAYANAGAR
1
BTS Depot
RASHTRIYA VIDYALAYA ROAD
THAYAPPANAHALLI
PTO
Quarters (BWSSB)
MARENAHALLI ROAD
2
MARENAHALLI
onut &
canut
tation
MARENAHALLI
AKKI
SARAKKI ROAD
J.P. NAGAR
(SARAKKI LAYOUT)
SARAKKI AGRAHARA
3
C
D

170
175

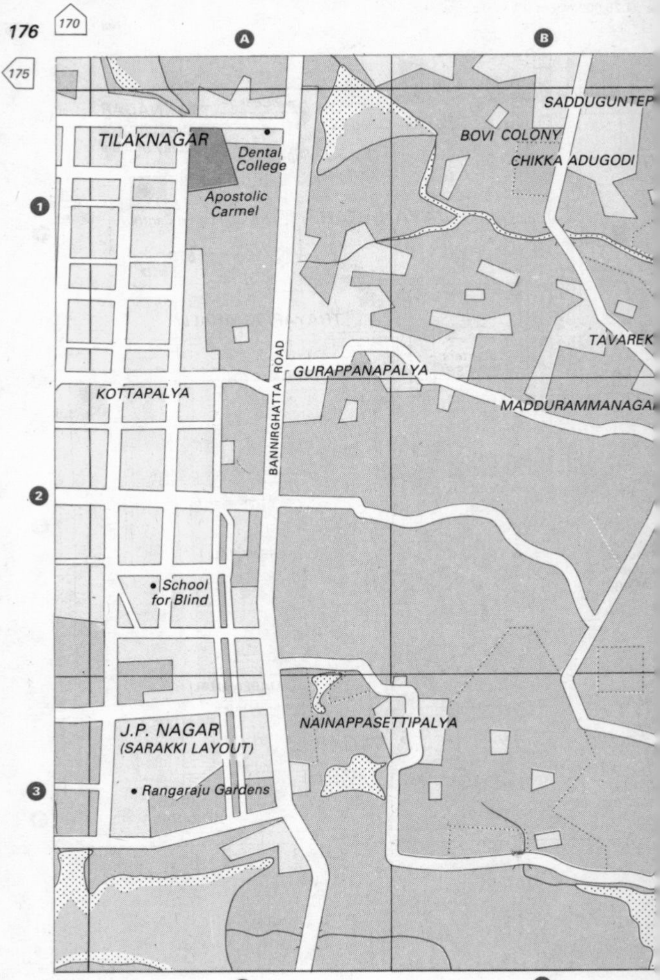

Based upon Survey of India map with the permission of the Surveyor General of India.

le : 1:25,000 (4 cm = 1 km)

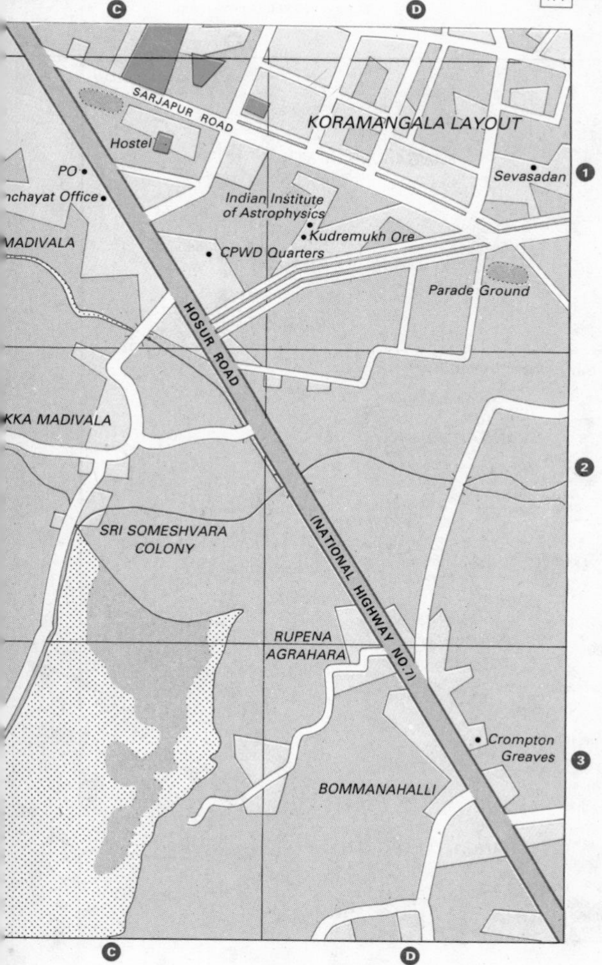

C
D
171
SARJAPUR ROAD
KORAMANGALA LAYOUT
Hostel
PO
nchayat Office
Sevasadan
1
Indian Institute
of Astrophysics
Kudremukh Ore
MADIVALA
CPWD Quarters
Parade Ground
HOSUR ROAD
KKA MADIVALA
2
SRI SOMESHVARA
COLONY
(NATIONAL HIGHWAY NO.7)
RUPENA
AGRAHARA
Crompton
Greaves
3
BOMMANAHALLI
C
D

Scale : 1:25,000 (4 cm = 1 km)

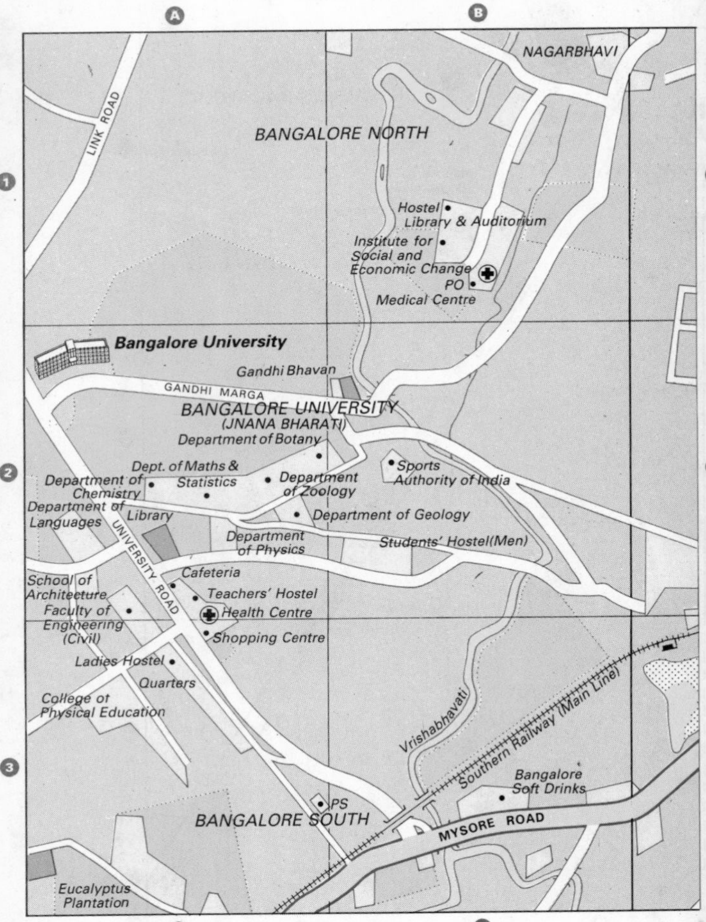

Based upon Survey of India map with the permission of the Surveyor General of India.

MYSORE
KEY TO MAPS

Scale: 1:110,000 (1 cm = 1.1 km)

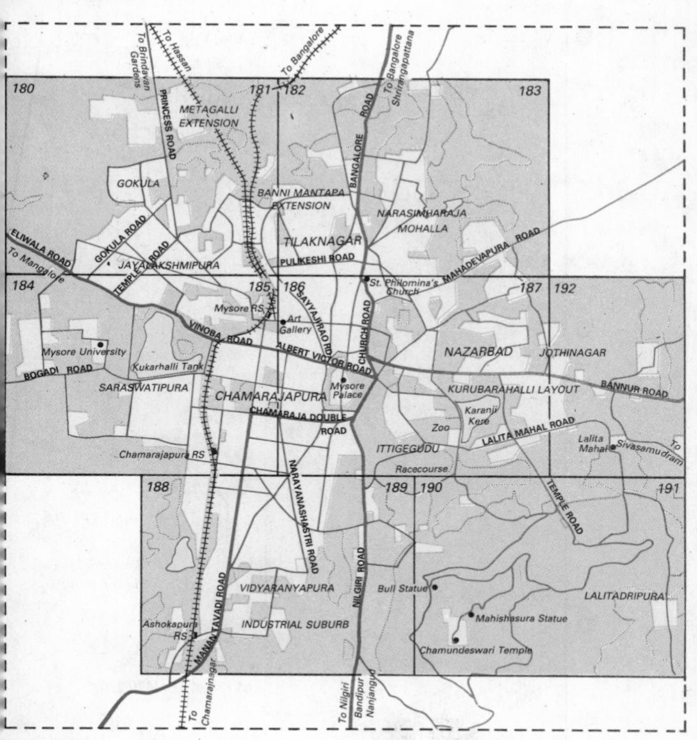

To Brindavan Gardens
To Hassan
To Bangalore
To Bangalore Shrirangapattana
180
181
182
183
PRINCESS ROAD
METAGALLI EXTENSION
BANGALORE ROAD
GOKULA
BANNI MANTAPA EXTENSION
NARASIMHARAJA MOHALLA
TILAKNAGAR
ELIWALA ROAD
To Mangalore
GOKULA ROAD
TEMPLE ROAD
JAYALAKSHMIPURA
PULIKESHI ROAD
MAHADEVAPURA ROAD
184
185
186
187
192
St. Philomina's Church
SAYYAJIRAO RD
Mysore RS
Art Gallery
CHURCH ROAD
VINOBA ROAD
ALBERT VICTOR ROAD
NAZARBAD
JOTHINAGAR
Mysore University
Kukarhalli Tank
BOGADI ROAD
SARASWATIPURA
CHAMARAJAPURA
Mysore Palace
KURUBARAHALLI LAYOUT
BANNUR ROAD
CHAMARAJA DOUBLE ROAD
Karanji Kere
Zoo
LALITA MAHAL ROAD
Lalita Mahal
To Sivasamudram
Chamarajapura RS
ITTIGEGUDU
Racecourse
188
189
190
191
NARAYANASHASTRI ROAD
TEMPLE ROAD
NILGIRI ROAD
VIDYARANYAPURA
Bull Statue
LALITADRIPURA
MANANTAVADI ROAD
Ashokapura RS
INDUSTRIAL SUBURB
Mahishasura Statue
Chamundeswari Temple
To Chamarajnagar
To Nilgiri
Bandipur
Nanjangud

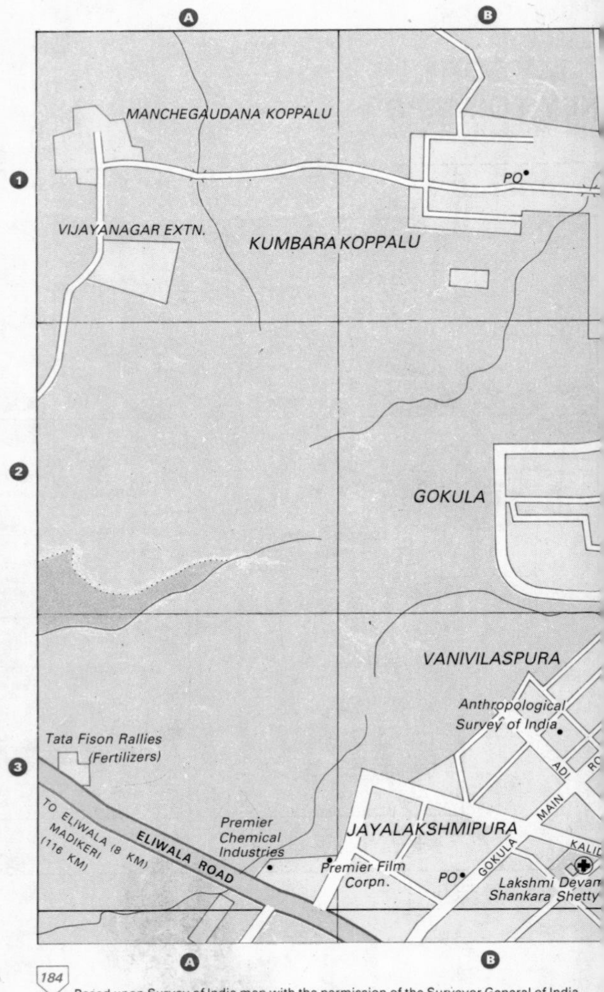

Based upon Survey of India map with the permission of the Surveyor General of India.

e : 1:25,000 (4 cm = 1 km)

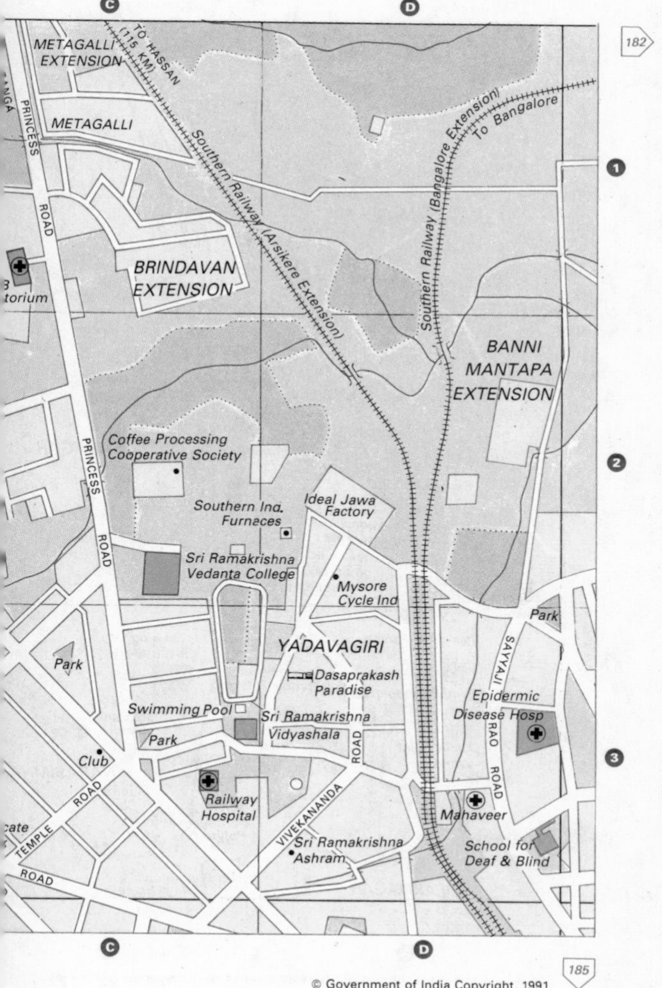

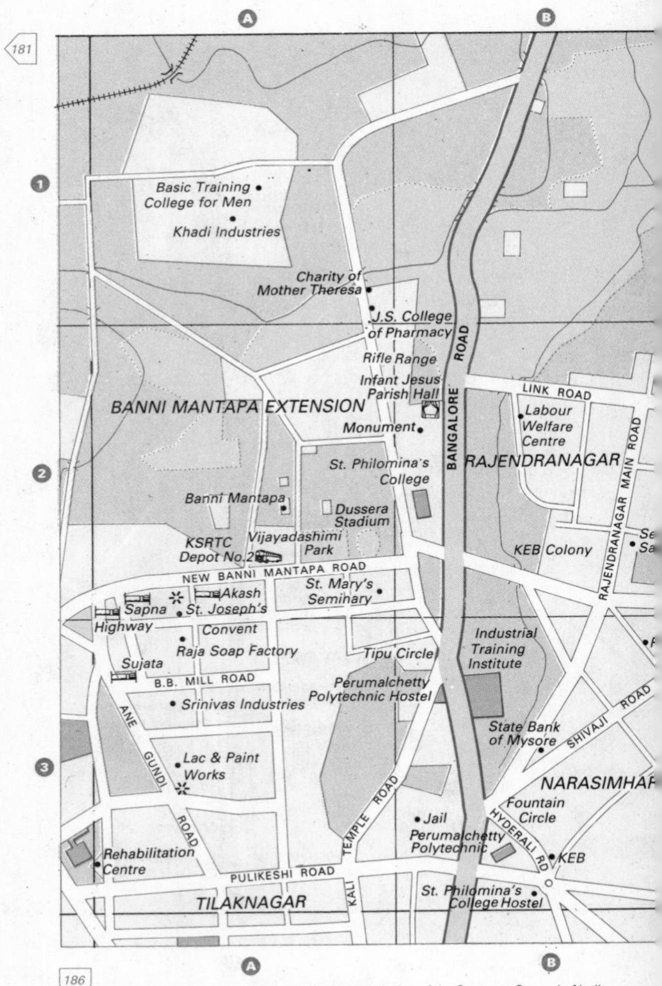
A
B
181
1
2
3
Basic Training College for Men
Khadi Industries
Charity of Mother Theresa
J.S. College of Pharmacy
Rifle Range
Infant Jesus Parish Hall
BANNI MANTAPA EXTENSION
Monument
BANGALORE ROAD
LINK ROAD
Labour Welfare Centre
RAJENDRANAGAR MAIN ROAD
RAJENDRANAGAR
St. Philomina's College
Banni Mantapa
Dussera Stadium
KSRTC Depot No.2
Vijayadashimi Park
KEB Colony
NEW BANNI MANTAPA ROAD
St. Mary's Seminary
Akash
Sapna
St. Joseph's Convent
Highway
Raja Soap Factory
Tipu Circle
Industrial Training Institute
Sujata
B.B. MILL ROAD
Perumalchetty Polytechnic Hostel
Srinivas Industries
ANE GUNDI ROAD
State Bank of Mysore
SHIVAJI ROAD
Lac & Paint Works
TEMPLE ROAD
NARASIMHA
Fountain Circle
Jail
HYDERALI RD
Perumalchetty Polytechnic
KEB
Rehabilitation Centre
PULIKESHI ROAD
KALI
St. Philomina's College Hostel
TILAKNAGAR
186

Based upon Survey of India map with the permission of the Surveyor General of India.

le : 1:25,000 (4 cm = 1 km)

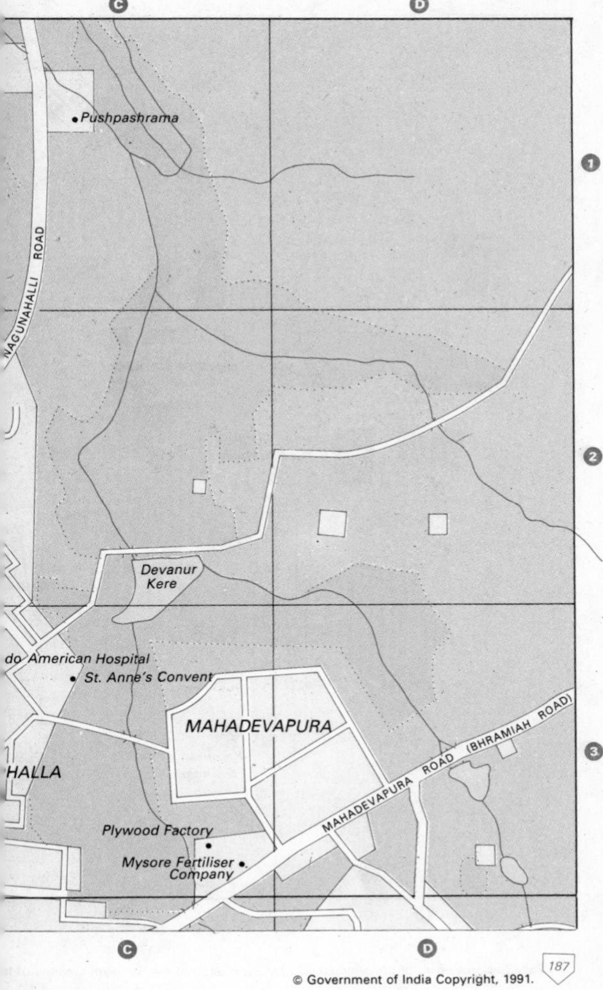

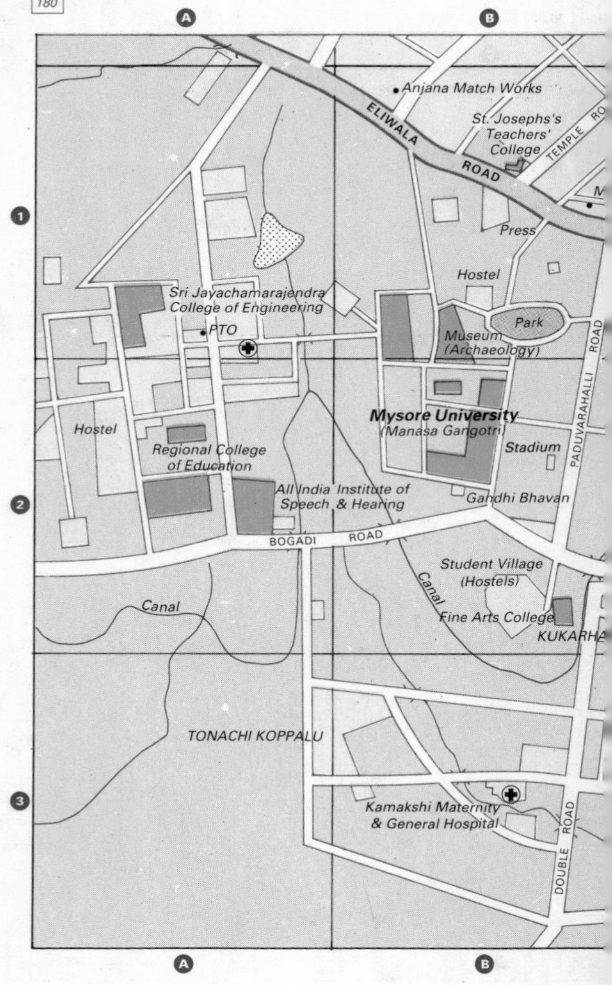

Based upon Survey of India maps with the permission of the Surveyor General of Ir

: 1:25,000 (4 cm = 1 km)

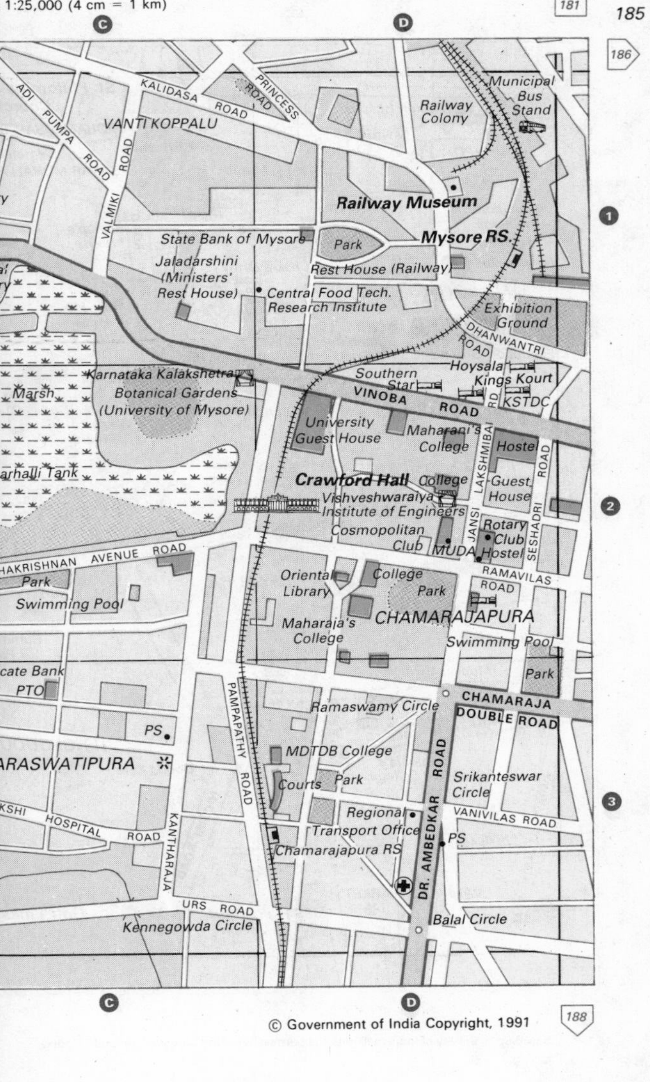

C
D
181
186
KALIDASA ROAD
PRINCESS ROAD
ADI PUMPA ROAD
VANTI KOPPALU
VALMIKI ROAD
Municipal Bus Stand
Railway Colony
Railway Museum
Mysore RS.
State Bank of Mysore
Park
Jaladarshini (Ministers' Rest House)
Rest House (Railway)
Central Food Tech. Research Institute
Exhibition Ground
DHANWANTRI ROAD
Marsh
Karnataka Kalakshetra
Botanical Gardens (University of Mysore)
Southern Star
Hoysala
Kings Kourt
KSTDC
VINOBA ROAD
University Guest House
Maharani's College
Hostel
LAKSHMIBAI RD
arhalli Tank
Crawford Hall
College
Guest House
Vishveshwaraiya Institute of Engineers
Cosmopolitan Club
MUDA
JANSI
Rotary Club
Hostel
SESHADRI ROAD
HAKRISHNAN AVENUE ROAD
Park
Swimming Pool
Oriental Library
College Park
RAMAVILAS ROAD
Maharaja's College
CHAMARAJAPURA
Swimming Pool
Park
cate Bank
PTO
PAMPAPATHY ROAD
Ramaswamy Circle
CHAMARAJA DOUBLE ROAD
PS
ARASWATIPURA
MDTDB College
Courts
Park
Srikanteswar Circle
DR. AMBEDKAR ROAD
KSHI HOSPITAL ROAD
Regional Transport Office
VANIVILAS ROAD
PS
KANTHARAJA
Chamarajapura RS
URS ROAD
Kennegowda Circle
Balal Circle
1
2
3
188

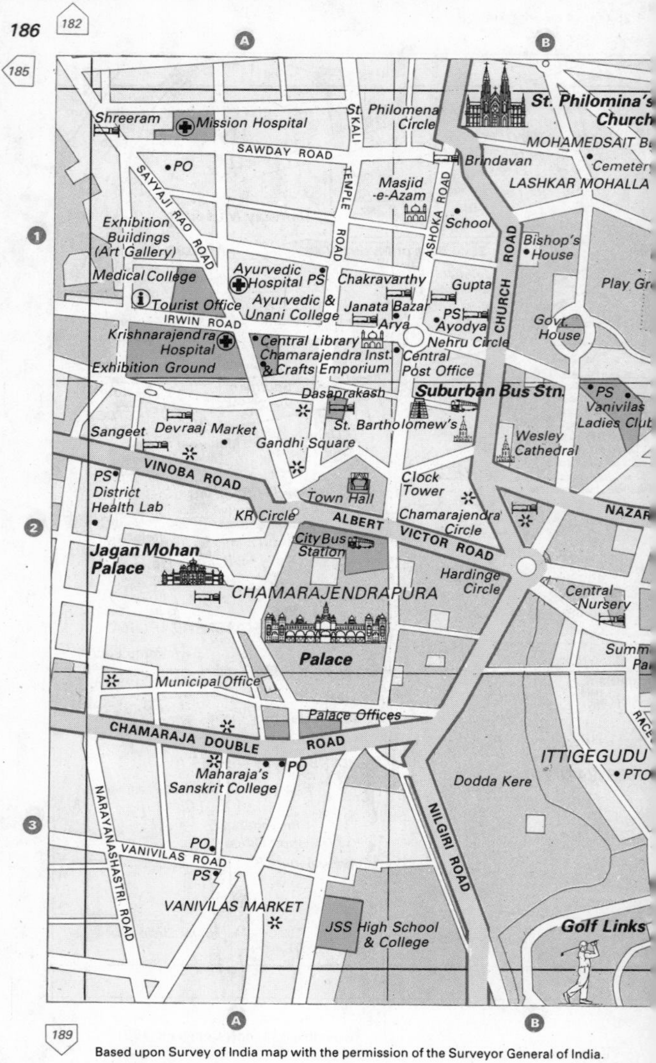

182

185

A
B
1
2
3

Shreeram
Mission Hospital
St. Philomena Circle
KALI TEMPLE ROAD
St. Philomina's Church
MOHAMEDSAIT B
SAWDAY ROAD
Brindavan
Cemetery
LASHKAR MOHALLA
PO
SAYYAJI RAO ROAD
Masjid -e-Azam
ASHOKA ROAD
School
Exhibition Buildings (Art Gallery)
CHURCH ROAD
Bishop's House
Medical College
Ayurvedic Hospital PS
Chakravarthy
Gupta
Play Gr
Tourist Office
Ayurvedic & Unani College
Janata Bazar
PS
Ayodya
Govt. House
IRWIN ROAD
Arya
Krishnarajendra Hospital
Central Library
Nehru Circle
Chamarajendra Inst. & Crafts Emporium
Central Post Office
Exhibition Ground
Dasaprakash
Suburban Bus Stn.
PS
Vanivilas Ladies Club
St. Bartholomew's
Sangeet
Devraaj Market
Gandhi Square
Wesley Cathedral
VINOBA ROAD
PS
District Health Lab
Clock Tower
Town Hall
KR Circle
ALBERT VICTOR ROAD
Chamarajendra Circle
NAZAR
City Bus Station
Jagan Mohan Palace
Hardinge Circle
CHAMARAJENDRAPURA
Central Nursery
Palace
Summ Pa
Municipal Office
Palace Offices
RACE
CHAMARAJA DOUBLE ROAD
PO
Maharaja's Sanskrit College
ITTIGEGUDU
PTO
Dodda Kere
NARAYANASHASTRI ROAD
NILGIRI ROAD
PO
VANIVILAS ROAD
PS
VANIVILAS MARKET
JSS High School & College
Golf Links

A
B

189

Based upon Survey of India map with the permission of the Surveyor General of India.

le : 1:25,000 (4 cm = 1 km)

183

192

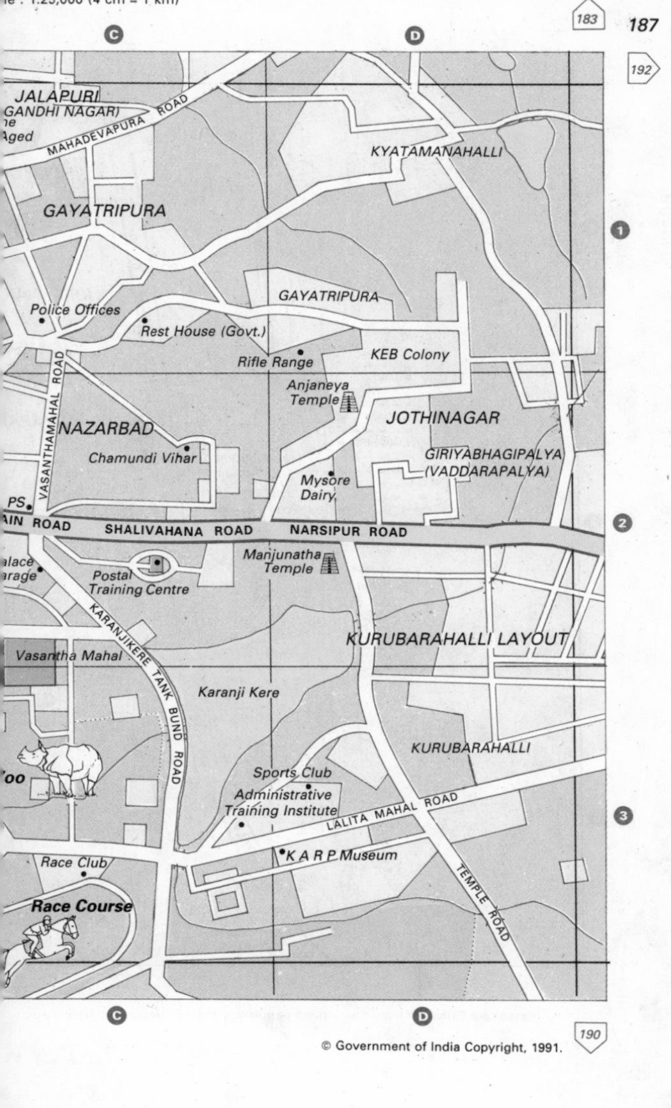

190

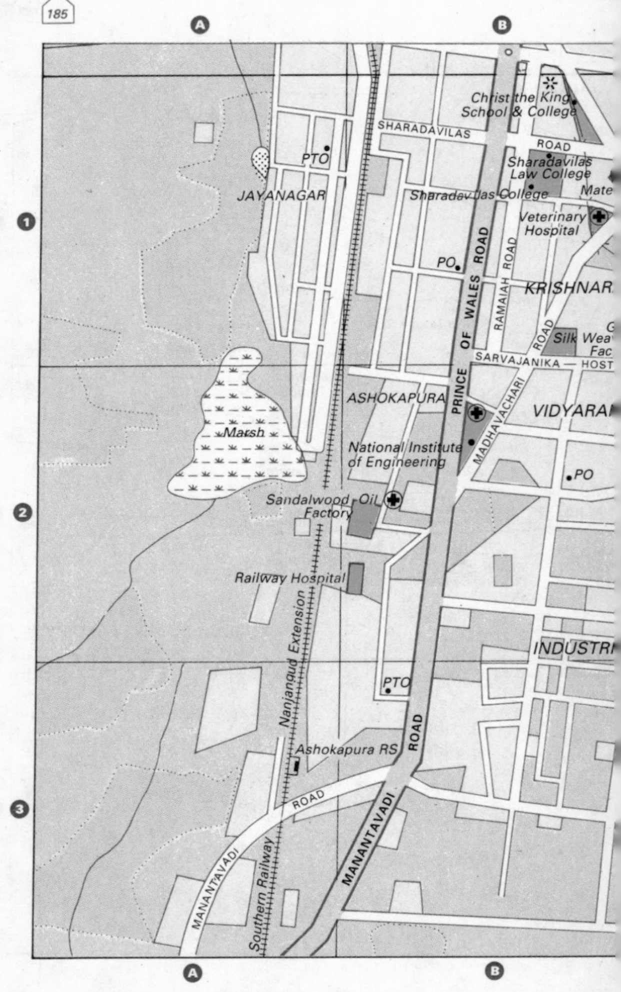

Based upon Survey of India map with the permission of the Surveyor General of India.

186

190

C
D
LAKSHMIPURA
NARAYANASHASTR
RAMANUJA ROAD
HARISHCHANDR ROAD
Golf Links
Madhuvana Dairy Farm
neral spital
PO
Betel
iculture Research & Training Institute
Gobli Tank
Preservation Centre
Karnataka Bank
JANSI LAKSHMIBAI ROAD
ROAD
J.S.S. College
CHAMUNDIPURA
NILGIRI ROAD
URB
Flour Mills
UDAGAMANDALAM (149 KM)
TO NANJANGUD (18 KM)
1
2
3

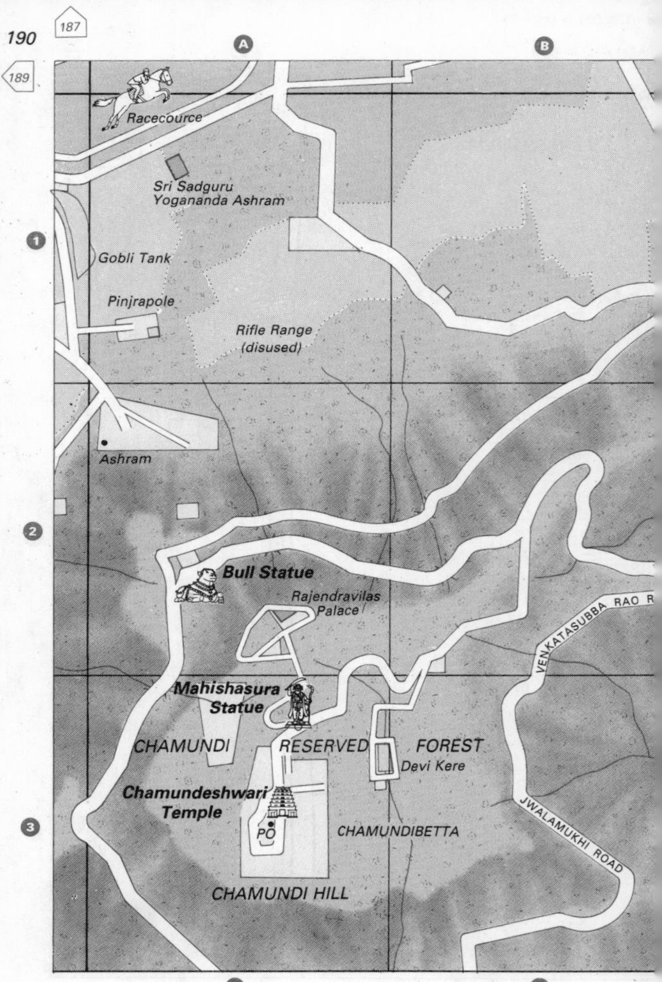

Based upon Survey of India map with the permission of the Surveyor General of India.

e : 1:25,000 (4 cm = 1 km)

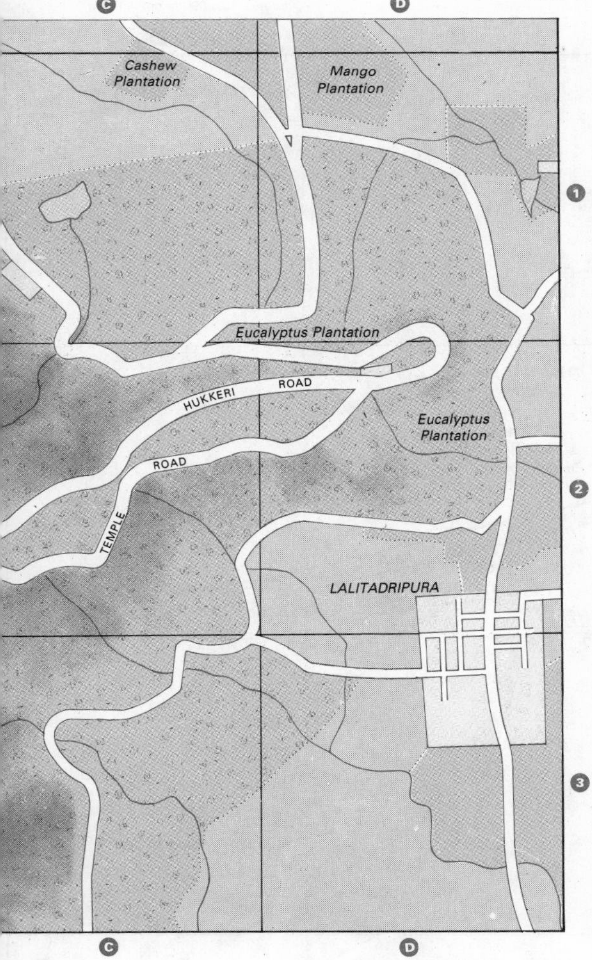

Scale : 1:25,000 (4 cm = 1 km)

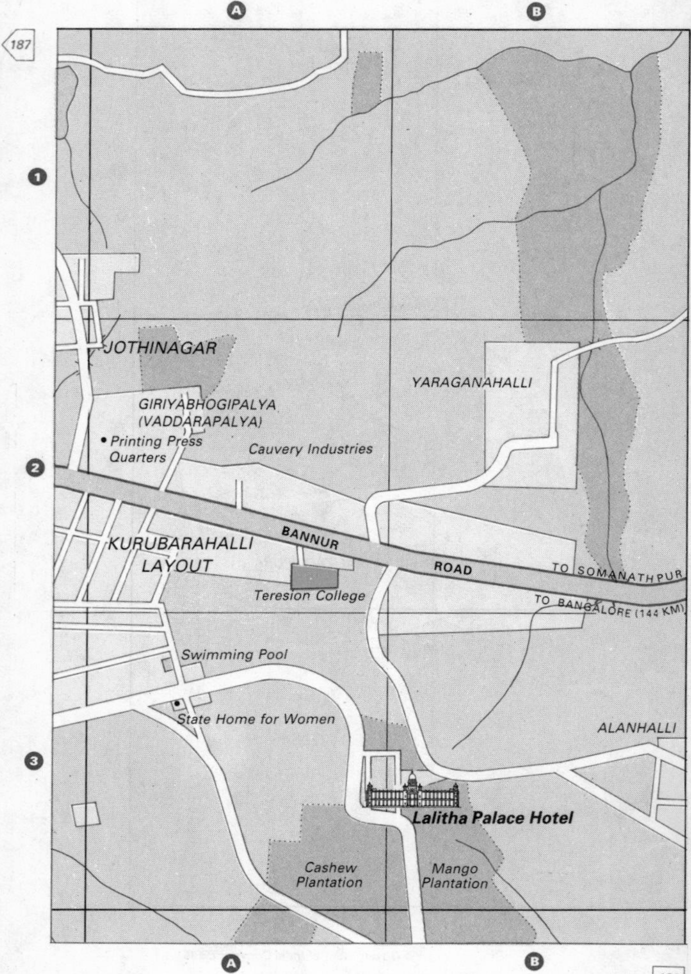

Based upon Survey of India map with the permission of the Surveyor General of India.

Text Index

Map Index

BANGALORE
STREET AND LOCALITY

(Note: References in italics indicate enlarged map of Central Bangalore on page 133)

MYSORE
STREET AND LOCALITY

AROUND BANGALORE – MYSORE